Günther & Yves Plamenig

THE INVISIBLE WALL

Why YouTube blocks you when you become interesting

Clarity about the cause

Publisher Bottom up

Notes:

Günther & Yves Plamenig

THE INVISIBLE WALL

Why YouTube blocks you when you become interesting

Clarity about the cause

Copyright: Bottom up Publishing House

Birkenstrasse 14

CH- 4142 Münchenstein - Switzerland

Email: bottomupverlag@gmail.com

1st edition

Unabridged edition:

January 2026 Bottom up Publishing

Cover page: Yves & Günther Plamenig

Typesetting: Yves Plamenig

Consulting: Marketing Yves Plamenig

Marketing: Yves and Günther Plamenig

Thanks to everyone who contributed to the publication of this book.

A special thank you to Yves once again.

Printing: Libri Plureos GmbH, Friedensallee 273, 22763 Hamburg

ISBN 978-3-907808-06-1 EAN 9783907808061

Notes:

Table of Contents:

Notes:

Introduction:

Reach doesn't disappear suddenly; it retreats quietly, almost imperceptibly, almost respectfully. Many creators experience this moment without being able to name it. The content becomes clearer, the thoughts more precise, the attitude more mature, and yet something begins to falter. Not because something has gotten worse, but because something has become more independent. YouTube does not respond to this change with errors, warnings, or explanations; it responds with silence. This book begins exactly where that silence sets in. For a long time, growth followed improvement. Those who improved became more visible, those who became more relevant were disseminated. This logic was simple, understandable, and deeply human. It no longer applies. Not because quality has been devalued, but because it is no longer what keeps the system stable. YouTube in 2026 is no longer a place of unbridled expansion; it is a regulating space, a system that does not maximize attention, but smooths it out. Attention is not a scarce commodity today; it is a risk. The stronger the impact of content, the more it changes perception, mood, and behavior.

The stronger creators become, the less predictable their effects become. And the less predictable something is, the more cautiously a system that has to balance billions of people at the same time reacts. Algorithms do not optimize creativity; they optimize predictability. Not out of malice, not out of ideology, but out of mathematical necessity. This book does not portray YouTube as an adversary; it describes YouTube as what it has become: an infrastructural nervous system of collective attention. In such a system, the goal is not what is interesting, but what is predictable.

Predictability creates stability, stability prevents fluctuations, and fluctuations threaten balance. That is why repetitions perform better than developments, why formats grow faster than ideas, and why depth is not prohibited, but dosed. Creators sense this dampening earlier than others, not because they fail, but because they are more sensitive. Those who create meaning create impact, and those who create impact are regulated. This explains why many channels stagnate even though their content matures, why growth suddenly no longer follows a linear path, and why authenticity sometimes feels like a disadvantage. This book is not a guide to conformity; it is an invitation to understanding. Because those who understand stop fighting and begin to position themselves correctly. YouTube does not block reach; it filters dynamics. It no longer measures clicks, but behavioral probabilities; not individual videos, but long-term patterns; not creativity, but controllability.

Those who don't recognize this logic unconsciously send the wrong signals. Those who do recognize it don't work against the system, but with its structure. This book doesn't promise tricks, it provides guidance. It combines platform economics, neuropsychology, AI logic, and cultural shifts into a clear picture that is neither simplistic nor didactic, but precise. It is aimed at creators who feel they have more to say but are less visible, at web video producers who do not want to compromise on quality in order to maintain reach, at everyone who has recognized that the old rules no longer apply, but the new ones are still unspoken. YouTube is not an enemy, it is a mirror. A mirror for collective attention, for social nervousness, for dealing with meaning in the digital space. Those who learn to read this mirror will grow not only as creators, but also as designers. Reach has not disappeared; it has only changed its conditions. And this is exactly where this book begins.

Notes:

Chapter 1: Why reach is no longer growing, even though everything is getting better

The moment when improvement is no longer visible

It rarely starts with a break, almost always with irritation. A quiet feeling that something is no longer right. The numbers still look stable, perhaps even respectable, but they are no longer responding. They do not respond to more care, better arguments, or more precise language. Videos become more thoughtful, calmer, often bolder, and yet the reach remains stagnant, as if it had decided to decouple itself from the development of content. This moment is not an isolated case. It is a pattern. And it marks the point at which many creators begin to doubt themselves, even though objectively speaking, the exact opposite has happened. They have gotten better. For a long time, improvement was visible. It had a clear counterpart on the outside. More clarity led to more resonance. More depth led to more engagement. More relevance led to more reach.

This logic was not only technical, it was culturally anchored. It corresponded to a deep human sense of justice. Those who make an effort should be allowed to grow. Those who learn should advance. Those who have something to say should be heard. For years, YouTube was the place where this idea seemed to be confirmed. Not perfect, not always fair, but fundamentally understandable. Improvement had an effect. But systems don't change because they want to, but because they have to. YouTube today is no longer the ecosystem it was ten years ago. It is not even the same as it was five years ago. It is a platform that has exceeded a critical size, beyond which growth is no longer just an opportunity, but a danger. A danger to stability, predictability, and control. And it is precisely at this moment that improvement begins to seem paradoxical. The moment when improvement is no longer visible is not a personal failure. It is a systemic transition. A transition from a phase in which creativity is enhanced to a phase in which it is restrained. Not openly, not ideologically, but functionally. The system changes long before anyone notices. And creators are the first to feel this change because they are the ones who move the most.

Improvement means change. Change means deviation. Deviation means uncertainty. For humans, uncertainty is a sign of development. For algorithms, it is a problem. Algorithms thrive on recognizability. They do not work with meaning, but with probabilities. They do not ask whether content is true, profound, or relevant. They ask how people behave after consuming this content. Do they remain predictable? Do they remain calm? Do they remain within familiar patterns? Or do they change their behavior in ways that are difficult to predict? In the early stages of a channel, this prediction is easy. New creators are clear. They send unambiguous signals. Their topics are focused, their language still raw, their impact limited. The system can quickly classify them. It can test, scale, compare. Growth feels like a natural reward at this stage. Many creators internalize this connection and consider it a rule. They believe that improvement automatically leads to greater visibility. They believe that quality will prevail if you just give it enough time.

This belief is understandable. But it is no longer correct. The break occurs when a channel begins to break away from its original template. When content no longer just works, but triggers something. When videos no longer just entertain, but set something in motion. This moment feels like a breakthrough for the creator. Finally, it's right. Finally, it feels complete. Finally, there is substance. But this is exactly where the system begins to become cautious. YouTube doesn't measure how good something is. It measures how stable the consequences are. A video that makes people think changes their emotional state. A video that shifts perspectives changes their clicking behavior. A channel that takes a stand changes expectations. These changes are not negative. But they are difficult to calculate. And what is difficult to calculate is dampened. Damping is not a ban. It is not a punishment. It is a reduction in expansion. Content is allowed to exist, but it is not allowed to spread uncontrollably. Reach is not withdrawn, it is limited. This is why many creators feel like they are running into an invisible wall. They give more, they get better, but they come up against a limit that is not visible and is not communicated. This limit is not a fixed number.

It is dynamic. It depends on topics, target groups, emotional intensity, and cultural context. It is constantly shifting. And that is precisely why it is so difficult to grasp. What worked yesterday seems to be slowing down today. What used to be considered progress is now causing hesitation. At this point, many creators begin to draw the wrong conclusions. They believe they need to correct themselves. They believe they have become too complex, too calm, too deep. They begin to simplify their content, tone down their statements, and smooth out their personalities. This often happens unconsciously. A slightly faster cut. A slightly more provocative title. A slightly clearer framing. In the short term, this can bring back reach. In the long term, however, an inner contradiction arises. The content moves away from what it actually wanted to be. The moment when improvement is no longer visible is so dangerous because it leads to self-denial. Not out of weakness, but out of ignorance. Those who do not understand why the system reacts differently interpret the reaction personally. They believe they are not good enough. Yet they have often reached the point where their content begins to become relevant. Relevance is not a loud state. It is often quiet. It takes time. It does not unfold its effect in a quick click, but in its reverberation. It is precisely this reverberation that the system finds difficult to represent. Algorithms are excellent at measuring immediate reactions. They are poor at capturing long-term shifts in meaning. That is why they prefer content whose effect is fast, clear, and limited. This shifts the focus of visible success. It no longer follows inner quality, but rather external fit. Fit between content and existing usage patterns. Fit between creator and target group profile. Fit between emotional intensity and systemic resilience. Those who fulfill this fit grow. Those who leave it behind are slowed down, regardless of how good they have become. This does not mean that development is pointless. On the contrary. Development is a prerequisite for long-term impact.

But it is no longer automatically visible. It runs below the surface of reach. It manifests itself in loyalty, in trust, in depth. These values are real, but they are no longer primarily scaled. The moment when improvement is no longer visible is therefore not the end. It is a transition. A transition from an external growth model to an internal one. From a phase of expansion to a phase of consolidation. Those who do not recognize this transition fight against the system. Those who recognize it begin to reposition themselves. This is exactly where this book comes in. Not with the question of how to regain reach, but with the question of why it has decoupled. Because only those who understand the reason can decide how to deal with it. Reach is no longer a measure of improvement. It is an indicator of system compatibility. This realization is uncomfortable. But it is liberating. Because it resolves the inner conflict. It explains why you get better and yet are seen less. It takes away the power of doubt. And it opens up space for a new form of growth. Growth that is not based on volume, but on clarity. Not on conformity, but on conscious readability. The moment when improvement is no longer visible is the moment when creators must decide how to proceed. Whether to conform to the system in order to become more visible again. Or whether they learn to be effective within the system in a different way. This decision is not moral. It is strategic. And it forms the foundation for everything that follows. This is where the first section ends. Not with a solution, but with an understanding. Because without this understanding, any strategy remains superficial. With it, however, a new way of thinking about reach, impact, and one's own role as a creator in 2026 begins.

Why development is considered a risk algorithmically

Development is a value in itself for humans. It stands for maturity, for learning, for the ability to endure complexity and integrate contradictions. Development means no longer being satisfied with simple answers, but asking questions that may remain open. It is precisely this quality that makes content truly meaningful for many creators. But what is experienced as progress by humans appears to an algorithmic system as a disruptive factor. Not because development is bad, but because it cannot be stabilized. Algorithms are not observers of meaning, but calculators of probability. They do not work with meanings, but with patterns. A pattern is valuable if it can be reproduced. The clearer a pattern, the easier it is to scale. Development, on the other hand, is the opposite of reproduction. It changes patterns. It shifts weightings. It breaks expectations.

This is precisely why it is algorithmically interpreted as a risk rather than a gain. In the early stages of a channel, this risk is low. Development takes place within a narrow framework. Small improvements, clearer language, better technology, more precise topic selection. This form of development remains readable. It does not change the basic structure of the channel, but optimizes it. The system can process this optimization because it does not jeopardize predictability. But at some point, a creator reaches a point where development is no longer just improvement, but transformation. And this is exactly where algorithmic caution begins. Transformation changes not only content, but also effects. It changes how people listen, how they react, how they feel after consumption.

A video that used to entertain begins to move people. A channel that used to inform begins to irritate. A creator who used to explain begins to question. These shifts are valuable from a human perspective. They create depth, relevance, and long-term loyalty. From a systemic perspective, however, they create variance. And variance is the enemy of any forecast. YouTube today is a system that not only distributes content, but also stabilizes behavior. It observes not only what people click on, but how they behave afterwards. They remain in similar emotional states. They switch between content in a controlled manner. Or they change their usage patterns in ways that are difficult to classify. Development creates precisely these effects that are difficult to classify. It makes users less predictable. And less predictable users increase the risk for the system. This risk is not abstract. It has concrete consequences.

A user who thinks differently, feels differently, or decides differently after watching a video is no longer a neutral consumer. They may be less responsive to classic triggers. They click more selectively. They linger differently. They are more difficult to classify into existing clusters. For the system, this means more computing power, more uncertainty, and more potential instability. That is why content that accompanies users rather than changing them is preferred. This is the core of the problem. Development changes people. And anything that changes people is systemically sensitive. Not because change is forbidden, but because it cannot be controlled. However, control is a prerequisite for scaling. A system that addresses billions of people at the same time must know what it triggers. It must be able to anticipate effects. Content whose impact is unknown eludes this logic. That is why development is algorithmically considered a risk. Not explicitly, not consciously, but implicitly. The system does not respond with a ban, but with restraint. It scales more cautiously. It tests longer. It limits reach without withdrawing it. For creators, this feels like stagnation. For the system, it is risk management. Many creators experience this moment as illogical. They feel like they have finally arrived, finally have something to say that goes beyond the surface. And at that very moment, their work loses visibility. This experience creates cognitive dissonance. Development should be rewarded. But this expectation is based on a human value system, not a technical one.

Algorithms do not know development curves. They only know deviations. Anything that no longer behaves exactly as before is reevaluated. This reevaluation is cautious. It begins with smaller tests, with limited playback, with narrower target groups. If the reactions remain stable, the reach can grow. If they vary, it is limited. Development almost always creates variability because it elicits new reactions. This creates a subtle pressure to adapt. Creators notice that content that changes too much gets less reach. They unconsciously learn what works. They learn which tone is preferred, which topics are safe, and what depth is accepted. This learning process is rarely conscious. It takes place gradually. But it influences decisions. It shapes content. It smooths out edges. The price of this adaptation is high. Not immediately, but in the long term. Content remains visible but loses its inner tension. It becomes efficient but interchangeable. Creators remain present but lose their development. The system becomes more stable, people become flatter. This exchange is not forced, but it is suggested.

Understanding development algorithmically as a risk does not mean giving it up. It means classifying its effect differently. Development is no longer a growth accelerator. It is a deep process. It does not automatically generate reach, but meaning. Meaning has a slower effect. It does not scale explosively, but sustainably. Many creators confuse this slowness with failure. They see stagnating numbers and believe they have lost touch. In reality, they have often reached a different level. A level that is no longer primarily defined by reach, but by resonance. Resonance is quieter than reach. But it is more stable. YouTube, however, is not designed to maximize resonance. It is designed to stabilize interaction. These two goals are not identical. Resonance can change people. Stability is meant to prevent that. That's why developing creators find themselves in a structural conflict of goals. They want to go deeper, while the system wants to remain shallow. This conflict cannot be resolved, but it can be navigated. The prerequisite for this is to recognize it. Those who believe that the system automatically rewards development will be disappointed. Those who understand that development is algorithmically considered a risk can make conscious decisions. They can decide how much risk they want to take.

How visible they want to remain. How much depth they allow. This does not mean censoring oneself. It means understanding one's own impact. Development creates responsibility. Responsibility means not only asking oneself what one wants to say, but also how it will be received. Not in the sense of conformity, but in the sense of clarity. This section marks another shift in perspective. Reach is no longer a reflection of one's own development. It is a reflection of systemic risk assessment. Those who understand this stop measuring development in terms of numbers. They begin to recognize it in terms of depth, consistency, and inner coherence. Why development is algorithmically considered a risk is not an accusation. It is a description. A description of the logic of a system that was not built for individual maturation, but for collective stability. Those who accept this logic can work within its limits without losing themselves. This is precisely where the next section comes in. Where it becomes apparent how quality itself can lose its reach, not because it gets worse, but because it does too much.

When quality loses its own reach

There is a point at which quality begins to turn against its own visibility. This point is difficult to pinpoint because it defies all classical logic. Quality should carry weight. Quality should convince. Quality should prevail. That is the cultural narrative deeply rooted in creative biographies. But in the context of YouTube 2026, this narrative loses its validity. Not because quality loses its value, but because it has a different kind of effect than the system can handle. Quality is not a neutral state. It is a condensation. It bundles attention, emotion, meaning, and attitude. The higher the quality, the stronger the effect. And it is precisely this effect that no longer automatically increases reach. Because today, reach is not the result of value, but of compatibility. A system that controls billions of people at the same time does not have to spread the best, but the most resilient. As quality increases, the character of content changes. It becomes not only more informative or aesthetic, but also more precise. Precision means exclusion. It sets boundaries. It no longer addresses everyone, but only those who are really listening. This is precisely where the decoupling of quality and reach begins. Reach thrives on breadth, while quality creates depth. Breadth is systemically easier to handle than depth. In the early stages of a channel, this tension is not noticeable. Quality and reach grow in parallel because quality is still generally accessible. It stays close to familiar patterns, common narratives, and trusted emotions. But as it matures, the focus shifts. Content becomes more specific.

Statements become clearer. Gray areas are no longer avoided but consciously entered. This development increases intrinsic value but reduces external scalability. YouTube responds to this shift not with rejection, but with limitation. The videos continue to be played, but in narrower clusters. They reach people who already think, feel, or search in similar ways. Reach stabilizes at a level that is considered safe. Growth beyond that is treated with caution. Not because it is impossible, but because it is not desired. This reveals a fundamental mechanism. Quality increases the intensity of the effect. Intensity creates variance. Variance increases risk. Risk is mitigated. This cycle is not moral, but functional. It explains why high-quality content often has a strong but limited impact.

It reaches fewer people, but it reaches them more deeply. Many creators experience this moment as an insult. They feel that their best work remains invisible. That videos they have put everything into are seen less than earlier, simpler content. This experience is painful because it contradicts their own value system. But it is not a sign of insignificance. It is a sign of relevance on a level that is no longer compatible with the masses. Quality does not lose its reach because it becomes worse, but because it becomes clearer. Clarity reduces connectivity. It forces positioning. It generates resonance instead of mere reaction. However, resonance is difficult to measure. It does not show up immediately in clicks, but in long-term loyalty, in trust, in inner movement. These effects are real, but they are systemically expensive. YouTube measures what is easy to measure: clicks, dwell time, interaction rates. It also measures secondary effects such as follow-up interactions and changes in usage paths. What it cannot measure well is significance. Significance unfolds over time. It has a lasting effect. It changes thought processes. These changes cannot be neatly translated into metrics. That is why they are not scaled. This creates a paradoxical situation. The higher the quality of content, the greater its potential for change.

The greater the potential for change, the more cautious the system. Quality is not punished, but rather contained. It is allowed to exist, but it must not spread uncontrollably. This mechanism explains why many high-quality channels have a strong core community but hardly grow beyond that. The content is too specific, too deep, too independent to be distributed en masse. The system recognizes this independence and limits its reach, not out of devaluation, but for reasons of stability. This creates an internal conflict for creators. They have to decide what they want. Visibility or depth. Breadth or precision. This decision is rarely conscious. It manifests itself in small adjustments. In the choice of topics. In the tone. In the question of whether to simplify something or leave it as it is. Each of these decisions influences how readable a piece of content remains for the system. Many creators try to circumvent this conflict by separating quality and reach. On the one hand, they produce accessible content for growth and, on the other hand, deeper content for themselves. This strategy may work in the short term, but it creates an internal divide. The channel loses coherence. The attitude becomes ambiguous. The system responds to this with further caution. Quality is not only what is said, but also how it is said.

It manifests itself in rhythm, language, pauses, nuances. These subtleties are noticeable to humans, but difficult for algorithms to classify. The more refined the content becomes, the less it fits into standardized categories. However, standardization is the basis of algorithmic distribution. When quality loses its own reach, it does not mean that it becomes ineffective. On the contrary. It has an even stronger effect where it lands. It generates loyalty instead of mere attention. It creates trust instead of mere interaction. These effects are more valuable in the long term than short-term reach. But they are not rewarded because they are not scalable. YouTube is not a space for cultural excellence, but for cultural balance. It must avoid extremes in order to remain stable. Quality is often an extreme because it cannot be smoothed out. It challenges. It contradicts. It irritates. It is precisely these qualities that make it valuable, but also risky. Many creators draw the wrong conclusion from this experience. They believe they have to reduce their quality in order to grow again. But the problem is not quality itself, but its translation. Quality that cannot be translated remains isolated.

Quality that does not reflect its own structure acts like a foreign body to the system. This section marks another turning point in the understanding of reach. Reach is no longer a measure of quality. It is a measure of system compatibility. Quality does not lose its reach because it is wrong, but because it is too powerful. Once you recognize this, you can stop tearing yourself between quality and visibility. They can begin to consciously shape quality. Not to water it down, but to make it legible. Legibility does not mean simplification. It means structure. It means rhythm. It means connectivity without self-betrayal. This is precisely where a new scope for action opens up. A space in which quality does not have to be abandoned, but is positioned differently. This space is narrow, but it exists. And it will become increasingly clear as this book progresses. Because when quality loses its own reach, it is not the end. It is a signal. A signal that you are moving along the boundary between impact and control. And it is precisely at this boundary that it will be decided how creators can grow in 2026 without losing themselves.

The invisible boundary between impact and control

There is a boundary that is not marked, that is not communicated, and yet it exists. It does not run between good and bad content, between permitted and prohibited topics, between large and small channels. This boundary runs between impact and control. It is the point at which content begins to have more impact than the system is prepared to bear. And it is the point at which reach is no longer expanded, but restricted. This boundary is invisible because it cannot be formulated as a rule. It is not a violation, not a mistake, not a reason for sanction. It is a state of equilibrium. As long as content has an impact without shifting the balance, it is disseminated. As soon as it begins to challenge this balance, its dissemination is limited. Not out of rejection, but out of caution. Control is not an instrument of power in the classical sense. Control is a prerequisite for scaling. YouTube 2026 is no longer a place where impact can grow unchecked. It is a system that doses impact. Dosing is necessary because impact is not linear. Content that touches ten people is not simply ten times as effective as content that touches one person. Impact is exponential. It is amplified by resonance, repetition, and context. And it is precisely this exponential growth that must be controlled. For creators, this limit is difficult to recognize because it is not evident in the content itself, but in its distribution.

A video feels right. It is coherent, clear, precise. The comments are profound, the feedback personal. Everything indicates that something significant has been achieved. And yet the reach remains limited. This paradox creates confusion because it contradicts the usual cause-and-effect thinking. The reason for this lies in the way systems evaluate impact. YouTube does not evaluate the content, but the consequences. Not the statement, but the reaction. Not the quality, but the change. Impact is problematic when it changes behavior. When it causes people to consume differently, click differently, prioritize differently. These changes are not negative per se. But they are difficult to calculate. And what is difficult to calculate is limited. In this context, control does not mean suppression, but predictability. A system that addresses billions of people at the same time needs to know what it triggers. It must ensure that extreme fluctuations do not destabilize the entire system.

That is why impact is not prohibited, but slowed down. It is allowed to unfold, but not explosively. This logic explains why content with a strong emotional or intellectual impact often has great depth but little breadth. It reaches exactly the people for whom it is relevant, but remains within that circle. The system recognizes the intensity and decides against massive scaling. Not because the content is wrong, but because its impact is not controllable enough. Many creators sense this limit without being able to name it. They feel that they are touching on something bigger than a single video. They notice that their content moves people. And at the same time, they notice that this very movement is not rewarded. This experience is frustrating because it contradicts their own aspirations. They want to make a difference and be seen for it. But the system separates these two levels. Impact is desirable as long as it remains controlled. Control means that impact follows familiar paths. That it fits into existing narratives. That it does not create new dynamics that are difficult to moderate. Content that irritates, questions, or breaks existing patterns quickly moves to this border. It is not prohibited. But it is treated with caution. This caution is no coincidence. It is the result of years of experience. Platforms have learned that uncontrolled impact creates side effects. Polarization, overload, emotional escalation, loss of trust. All these phenomena did not arise from individual pieces of content, but from their mass dissemination. The answer to this is not censorship, but regulation.

And today, this regulation takes place algorithmically. The invisible line between impact and control is constantly shifting. It depends on the social climate, political tensions, and cultural trends. In times of high uncertainty, it narrows. In more stable phases, it widens. Creators who operate close to this boundary feel these shifts particularly strongly. Their reach fluctuates, not because they work inconsistently, but because the system reacts more sensitively. This sensitivity does not only affect political or social issues. It also affects personal development, education, psychology, spirituality, everything that moves people internally. The more a piece of content contributes to people reflecting on their thoughts, feelings, or actions, the closer it comes to this boundary. And the more cautious its distribution becomes. For many creators, this realization is sobering. They had hoped that depth could be a driver of growth.

Instead, they experience depth as a limitation. But this perception is only paralyzing if reach is considered the sole goal. However, if reach is understood as one of several levels, the perspective changes. The boundary between impact and control is not an obstacle, but a marker of orientation. It shows where content begins to become relevant. It marks the transition from entertainment to meaning. Those who reach this boundary have created something that has an impact. The question is not how to break through this boundary, but how to position oneself at it. Positioning means becoming aware of one's own impact. Understanding which topics, which tone, which depth one creates. And accepting that not every impact is suitable for the masses. This does not mean giving up on growth. It means defining growth differently. Many creators try to ignore the boundary between impact and control. They continue to produce as if it did not exist. They increase intensity, polarize more strongly, provoke more consciously. In the short term, this can generate attention. In the long term, however, it leads to even stricter regulation. The system responds to boundary violations not with openness, but with tighter limits. The alternative is not conformity, but awareness. Those who understand where this boundary lies can decide how close they want to get to it. They can design content in such a way that it has an impact without being overwhelming. That it has depth without becoming chaotic.

That it asks questions without destabilizing the system. This balance is challenging. It requires clarity, structure, and a deep understanding of one's own impact. But it is possible. And it is the key to sustainable growth in a system that prioritizes stability over expansion. The invisible boundary between impact and control is not a sign of limitation, but of maturity. It shows that content has reached a level where it is no longer just consumed, but processed. Those who recognize this boundary can use it. Not to break it, but to work along its line. This is where the focus shifts. Away from the question of how to force reach. Toward the question of how to shape impact responsibly. This shift is subtle, but it changes everything. It resolves the inner struggle between depth and visibility. It enables a new form of presence. The next section concludes this thought. It shows why stagnation is not a standstill, but a sign of regulation. And why this regulation in particular conceals a new growth model.

Why stagnation is not stagnation, but regulation

Stagnation is one of the most misunderstood phenomena in the life of a creator. It is almost always interpreted as failure, as a sign that something is no longer working, that one's work has lost relevance, or that one has missed the boat. This interpretation is humanly understandable, but in most cases it is wrong. In the context of YouTube 2026, stagnation is not an expression of standstill. It is an expression of regulation. And regulation is not a coincidence, but an active state of the system. Standstill implies passivity. Regulation, on the other hand, is an intervention. It is the result of an assessment that is not openly communicated but is nevertheless effective. When reach stagnates, it does not mean that the system is doing nothing. It means that it is doing something very specific. It limits expansion in order to maintain balance. This distinction is crucial because it shifts the focus from one's own powerlessness to the logic of the system. YouTube does not regulate content, but dynamics. It does not respond to individual videos, but to patterns.

Stagnation is the result of pattern recognition that says further growth would create more uncertainty than benefit. This assessment is not final. It is situational. It can change. But it is effective at the moment it is made. Many creators experience stagnation as emptiness. The numbers hardly move. Comments remain constant. No new viewers are added. Everything feels frozen. But beneath this surface, the system is working intensively. It observes, tests, compares. It analyzes not only how content performs, but how it fits into the overall structure of the platform. Stagnation is often a phase of observation. A phase in which the system checks whether further opening is responsible. This phase can last a long time. Weeks, months, sometimes years. And that is precisely where its psychological difficulty lies. Humans are not built for long periods without visible feedback. We need feedback to maintain motivation. Stagnation deprives us of this feedback. It forces creators to continue working without external confirmation. That is exhausting. And that is precisely why many give up or adapt at this point. Adaptation provides short-term relief. It often gets the numbers moving again. But it comes at a price. It shifts the inner focus away from meaning and toward measurability. Content is designed to work better again, not necessarily to remain consistent. This shift is rarely conscious. It happens gradually. But it changes the inner relationship to one's own work. Understanding stagnation as regulation fundamentally changes this dynamic. When stagnation is not a sign of loss of value, but of systemic caution, it loses its threatening significance. It becomes a signal. A signal that content has reached a level of impact that is no longer automatically scaled.

This is not a step backward. It is a transition. Regulation kicks in when growth no longer means just expansion, but influence. Influence is always ambivalent. It can enrich, but it can also destabilize. Platforms have learned that uncontrolled influence carries long-term risks. That's why influence is measured out. And this measurement manifests itself as stagnation. Many creators believe they have to overcome this phase in order to grow again. In reality, this phase is often a prerequisite for a different kind of growth. Growth that is not based on mass, but on density. Density means that the impact per viewer increases. That fewer people are reached, but more intensively. This form of growth is not visible in traditional metrics, but it is real. YouTube measures this density only to a limited extent. It recognizes engagement, but it cannot fully reflect depth. That is why this form of growth often remains invisible.

But it is this growth that enables long-term stability. Channels that survive this phase develop an inner robustness. They are less dependent on short-term fluctuations. They have a clearer profile.

They know what they stand for. Regulation is also a protective mechanism. It protects creators from growing too big too quickly. Rapid growth can be overwhelming. It increases pressure to meet expectations, comparisons, and the need to conform. Many channels that grow explosively disappear just as quickly. Stagnation slows down this process. It forces consolidation. This consolidation is uncomfortable, but valuable. It gives space to consolidate one's own voice. It allows content to be deepened without having to react immediately to numbers. It separates intrinsic motivation from extrinsic motivation. Those who continue in this phase do so primarily for the sake of the cause itself, rather than for the sake of reach. This changes the quality of the work. However, regulation is no guarantee of future growth. It is a condition. Whether it leads to new reach depends on how creators deal with it. Those who experience it as stagnation will try to break through it. Those who understand it as regulation will use it. Using it does not mean becoming passive, but working consciously. Not simplifying content, but structuring it. Not reducing depth, but making it more accessible. Stagnation is often the point at which it is decided whether a channel will become a long-term project or a short-term experiment. Looking back, many successful creators report long phases of apparent insignificance. Phases in which nothing progressed. These phases were not empty. They were formative.

They laid the foundation for later breakthroughs that were more stable than any early growth. YouTube does not regulate arbitrarily. It regulates to stabilize patterns. When a channel shows that it remains consistent even in phases of low expansion, its systemic trustworthiness increases. Trust is not a human concept, but a statistical one. It means that a channel remains predictable even as it grows. This predictability is the prerequisite for renewed openness.

Stagnation is therefore often a test. Not a moral one, but a structural one. It tests whether a channel is viable even without expansion. Whether it has substance. Whether it is designed not only for growth, but also for impact. This test is hard because it has no clear end. But it is crucial. Those who understand stagnation as regulation can remain calm inside. They stop analyzing every fluctuation.

They stop comparing themselves to others. They begin to follow their own path. This calmness is palpable. It changes tone, tempo, presence. And it is precisely these changes that can enable growth again in the long term because they stabilize the impact. Regulation does not mean that growth is impossible. It means that growth is being prepared. Not in numbers, but in structure. Most large, long-lasting channels have not grown continuously. They have experienced plateaus. Long, tough plateaus. These plateaus were not pauses. They were phases of consolidation. During these phases, what is essential becomes clear. Topics are sorted. Formats mature. One's own voice becomes clearer. This clarity is not loud.

It is calm. But it is sustainable. And sustainability is what systems accept in the long term. Understanding why stagnation is not stagnation but regulation changes the internal approach to reach. It loses its absolute value. It becomes one of many signals. A signal of where you stand. Not in comparison to others, but in relation to your own impact. Chapter one ends here because at this point, the foundation has been laid. Reach no longer grows automatically with improvement. Development is seen as a risk. Quality can lose its own reach. Impact meets control. And stagnation proves to be an active state, not a void. Those who understand these five connections will look at YouTube differently. Not as a stage on which you have to prove yourself, but as a system in which you position yourself. This understanding is the prerequisite for everything else.

Without it, any strategy remains superficial. With it, however, it becomes clear why growth will be different in 2026. Chapter two picks up exactly here. It shows how YouTube has quietly and invisibly realigned itself. And why almost no one recognized this change in time.

Notes:

Notes:

Chapter 2: YouTube's quiet realignment

The platform that changed without saying so

Platforms never change where you can see them. They change where no one is looking. Not in public announcements, not in creator updates, not in new features, but in quiet shifts in their internal logic. YouTube is the most precise example of this. The platform has changed fundamentally since 2023 without ever openly acknowledging this change. Not out of deception, but because it cannot be communicated without questioning its own self-image. YouTube continues to talk about creativity, community, and opportunities. These terms are not wrong, but they are no longer complete. They stem from a phase when growth still meant expansion. When reach was a promise. When visibility worked as a reward.

But that phase is over. Not officially, but structurally. The change did not begin with a decision, but with a necessity. YouTube became too big to be left to its own devices. Too influential to remain neutral. Too effective to just distribute. As its reach grew, so did its responsibility, not in a moral sense, but in a systemic one. Any platform that crosses a certain threshold goes from being a marketplace to infrastructure. And infrastructure must be stable. Stability is not a creative value. It is a technical one. It requires predictability, consistency, and the dampening of extremes. This is precisely where YouTube's quiet realignment begins. Away from an open distribution system, toward a regulating space for attention. This shift was not announced because it is not a feature. It is a new mode of operation. YouTube used to be an amplifier. Content that generated resonance was passed on. The algorithm was an accelerator. Today, YouTube is a filter. Content is not primarily amplified, but classified. Not everything that works is disseminated. Only what fits into the current stability model. This change took place gradually. Small adjustments to recommendation logic.

New weightings of signals. Changed test phases. Extended observation periods. No single measure was drastic enough to trigger resistance. But taken together, they have realigned the platform. Creators who have been around for a long time feel this change most strongly. They remember a time when experimentation was rewarded. When disruption generated attention. When independence was a driver of growth. Today, that same independence has a dampening effect. Not because it is wrong, but because it is more difficult to classify. YouTube has learned that unchecked momentum has side effects. Not only politically or socially, but also psychologically. Overwhelm, polarization, exhaustion. Users who see too much at once tune out. They leave the platform or become unpredictable. Both are problematic. That's why the goal has shifted.

No longer maximum attention, but sustainable use. Sustainability sounds harmless. But it changes everything. It means that content must no longer just be exciting, but also acceptable. Acceptable for users, for advertising models, for regulatory frameworks. Content that has too strong an impact jeopardizes this acceptability. It is not removed, but it is moved more slowly. This new logic explains many phenomena that creators cannot classify. Why videos with high watch time don't grow. Why comments are deep, but reach remains limited. Why old formats suddenly perform better than new ideas. These are all symptoms of a platform that no longer accelerates, but balances. YouTube 2026 is no longer a place where anything is possible, but a place where everything is classified. Classification means that content is given its place, but not necessarily the largest possible one. This place is not based on quality, but on system compatibility. YouTube's quiet realignment has a decisive consequence. It shifts responsibility. Previously, it lay with the creator. If you wanted to grow, you had to get better. Today, it lies with the system. Growth is granted, not earned. This is a fundamental difference. It explains why many creators feel powerless despite their high level of competence. This powerlessness is not a personal problem. It is a structural one. It arises when old performance logics encounter new control mechanisms. Those who continue to believe that visibility is the result of effort find themselves in an inner conflict. Because effort is no longer rewarded proportionally. The platform has changed without saying so because it had to change. And that is precisely why so few have recognized it.

Change without language remains invisible. It only manifests itself in effects. In shifts. In friction. In stagnation. This section makes one thing clear. If you want to understand YouTube today, you can no longer listen to what is being said. You have to observe what is happening. Not in individual cases, but in patterns. In long-term developments. In collective experiences. YouTube is no longer what it used to be. And it will never return to that. This realization is uncomfortable, but necessary. Because only when it is clear that the platform has fundamentally changed does it become understandable why old strategies no longer work. Chapter two therefore does not begin with numbers or features, but with a change of perspective. YouTube has realigned itself. Quietly. Profoundly. Irreversibly. And those who fail to recognize this change are working against a logic that no longer exists.

Why almost no one recognized the change in time

YouTube's transformation was not an event, but a process. That is precisely why it remained invisible to most people. People are trained to recognize change when it is clearly marked. New rules, new interfaces, new prohibitions. But systems rarely change in this way. They change through shifts in emphasis, adjustments in priorities, small corrections that seem harmless on their own but, taken together, create a new reality. YouTube chose this path not out of calculation, but out of necessity. Almost no one recognized the change in time because there was no clear moment when one could say, “Now everything is different.” Instead, much remained the same on the surface. The interface looked familiar. The platform's language remained optimistic. Creators were still encouraged to be creative, post regularly, and nurture their community.

None of this was untrue, but it was incomplete. Because while the narrative remained stable, the underlying logic changed. People orient themselves by language. What is not said does not exist for many people. YouTube never said that reach would be redefined. It never said that stability had become more important than expansion. It never said that impact had to be measured. Instead, individual signals were adjusted. A slightly different recommendation system. A new weighting of user satisfaction. An extended test phase for videos. None of these measures was spectacular enough to raise alarm bells. Added to this is a psychological effect.

Creators who have been successful for a long time have learned to trust their experience. They have recognized patterns, developed strategies, and reproduced successes. This knowledge was valid for a long time. And that is precisely why it became a trap. Because once you have learned how something works, you often realize too late that it has stopped working that way. Past success creates blindness to structural changes. YouTube's transformation also coincided with a period of constant change. New platforms, new formats, new trends. TikTok, shorts, livestreams, AI tools. Everything was moving at once. This dynamic obscured the actual change. Many creators interpreted declining reach as a competition problem. They believed that attention was being redistributed. That wasn't wrong, but it wasn't the core issue. The core issue was a change in the control logic within YouTube itself. Another reason for the delayed realization lies in the way algorithms are communicated. YouTube talks about recommendations, personalization, and user interests. These terms suggest neutrality. They convey the impression that content simply ends up where it belongs.

What is concealed is the normative character of these processes. Recommendations are not a reflection of interests, but decisions about probabilities. And these decisions follow goals that are not publicly discussed. Almost no one recognized the change because it was not communicated as a change, but as optimization. Optimization sounds like improvement. Like fine-tuning. Like something that supports existing goals. But in reality, the goal itself was shifted. From maximum attention to controlled attention. From growth at any price to sustainable use. This shift was not loud, but quiet. And quiet things are overlooked. Creators are also in a structural relationship of dependency. They depend on the platform to be visible. This dependency makes critical distance difficult. Those who live off the system rarely question it. Instead, they look for the cause of problems within themselves. They optimize, experiment, adapt. This self-focus obscures the view of systemic causes. Losses in reach are individualized, even though they occur collectively.

Another obstacle was the time lag in the effects. The change did not take effect immediately. Many channels continued to grow, even though the logic had already changed. Old content continued to perform well. Established formats were still being played out. This created the illusion of continuity. Only new content, new ideas, and new developments encountered invisible boundaries. But these boundaries were not recognized as systemic, but as personal setbacks. The diversity of experiences also contributed to the confusion. While some channels stagnated, others exploded. While some creators lost reach, others gained it. This inconsistent picture made it difficult to draw clear conclusions. But that is precisely where the clue lies. Systems that regulate do so selectively. They do not limit everything, but rather control it. Growth does not disappear, it is redistributed. This redistribution follows criteria that are difficult to identify from the outside. The change also went unnoticed because it did not create a clear winner-loser structure.

There was no open rupture, no obvious discrimination against certain groups. Instead, a diffuse state emerged. Many creators felt slowed down, but no one could say exactly why. This uncertainty led to speculation, myths, and recriminations. Shadow bans were suspected, secret limits, hidden rules. But all these explanations fall short because they are based on an outdated image of the platform. YouTube is no longer a neutral marketplace. It is a curated space. This curation is not content-based, but dynamic. It does not affect what is said, but how widely it spreads. This form of control is difficult to recognize because it does not intervene visibly.

It works in the background, in probabilities, in weightings. Those who have not learned to think in these categories overlook them. Almost no one recognized the change in time because it would have required a rethink. A rethink away from performance and toward impact. Away from visibility and toward stability. Away from growth and toward compatibility. These terms were not present in the creator discourse for a long time. They contradicted the self-image of a platform that presented itself as a place of opportunity. There is also a cultural factor. Success stories are louder than quiet shifts. The few channels that grew strongly dominated perception. They were seen as proof that everything was still working. That you just had to find the right strategies. But these stories were exceptions, not the rule. They obscured the systemic trend instead of making it visible. It was only when the stagnation became more widespread, when it no longer affected individuals but entire segments, that something began to stir. Educational channels, deep-dive formats, reflective content. Similar experiences everywhere.

Good content, stable communities, but limited reach. This collective pattern is the key to understanding. Individual deviations are coincidental. Collective shifts are systemic behavior. The change remained invisible for a long time because it did not cause a scandal. Scandals attract attention. They generate resistance. The change at YouTube merely created friction. Quiet friction. And friction is often perceived as a personal problem, not a structural one. People believe that they just need to try harder to overcome it. But friction is a signal. It shows that a system is no longer designed for acceleration. It shows that movement is no longer possible without restraint. In technical systems, friction is a means of stabilization. It prevents overheating. It protects against loss of control. YouTube introduced friction without naming it. And that is precisely why it was misunderstood for so long. This section makes it clear why the change was not obvious. It was too quiet, too diffuse, too complex.

It contradicted familiar explanations. It did not fit into familiar narratives. And it required thinking that went beyond individual strategies. Those who recognize the change today often do so in retrospect. They recognize patterns that previously seemed fragmented. They understand that the platform did not turn against creators, but had to protect itself. This realization is sobering, but it is clarifying. It ends the search for culprits. It ends the hope for simple solutions. Chapter two thus shows not only what has changed, but also why it took so long to see this change. And it is precisely this understanding that is crucial. Because only those who recognize that the rules have changed can stop searching for answers that come from a different time.

The new logic behind recommendations and limitations

To understand what actually drives YouTube today, you have to let go of the idea that recommendations are a neutral match between content and interest. This idea was never entirely correct, but it was functional enough to carry on for a long time. In 2026, it will finally be obsolete. Today, recommendations are no longer a reaction, but a preliminary decision. They are not primarily based on what users want, but on what the system considers viable. This shift is subtle, but it changes the core of the platform. Previously, recommendations followed the logic of resonance. Content was tested, reactions measured, distribution adjusted. The algorithm learned from user behavior and reinforced what worked.

This model was dynamic, open, and comparatively risk-tolerant. It accepted fluctuations because growth was the overriding goal. The larger the platform became, the less it could afford to be risk-tolerant. Today, YouTube follows a different logic. Recommendations are part of a stabilization system. They no longer serve primarily to maximize content visibility, but to regulate usage patterns. This means that not every video that works is automatically scaled. Today, scaling is a conscious decision by the system, not an automatic effect of performance. This decision is based on several levels that are rarely considered in isolation. It's not just about watch time or interaction rates, but about context. What is the user's emotional state? How consistent is their previous behavior? How much does the content deviate from what they usually consume? What follow-up content is likely to follow? Every recommendation is part of a chain, not a single moment. This is precisely where limitations arise. A piece of content can perform excellently and still not be recommended if its effect is considered too disruptive. In this context, disruptive does not mean provocative or controversial, but rather changing. Anything that shifts existing usage paths too much is treated with caution. The system prefers continuity over surprise. This new logic explains why recommendations often seem conservative today. Users see more of what they already know.

New impulses are dosed. Surprises are filtered out. The goal is not boredom, but stability. A stable user is a predictable user. A predictable user is easier to retain. And user retention is more important today than reach expansion. Limitations are not a side effect, but an active tool. They prevent individual content from becoming too big too quickly. They ensure that attention is distributed more evenly. They reduce peaks to ensure long-term use. These mechanisms are not visible because they are not communicated as restrictions. They appear to be a natural development of the platform. This logic is difficult for creators to accept because it contradicts their own aspirations. They want to grow with good content. They want to be seen. But visibility is no longer a right today, but a variable. It is given, not earned. And it is limited as soon as it becomes systemically problematic. Recommendations therefore no longer work linearly. A video can be played heavily in one target group and hardly at all in another. A channel can grow in certain phases and stagnate in others without any change in quality. This non-linearity is not a bug. It is the result of a system that seeks to balance rather than maximize. Another aspect of this new logic is the time delay. Recommendations no longer respond immediately. Content is observed for longer before it is scaled. The system collects data, checks effects, and evaluates stability. For creators, this feels like uncertainty. For the system, it is risk minimization. Quick successes are viewed with suspicion because they are often accompanied by sharp fluctuations. This delay changes the feeling of work. In the past, it was relatively easy to see whether a video was working. Today, this feedback is often lacking.

Success is no longer immediately visible. This creates frustration, but also a new kind of selection. Those who work only for quick validation lose motivation. Those who think long-term stay. The new logic behind recommendations and limitations is therefore not only technical but also culturally effective. It shapes what is produced. It influences what content is worthwhile. It favors consistency over experimentation. It rewards recognizability over development. These effects are not planned, but they are real. YouTube has thus become a space where not everything that is possible is visible. Visibility is the result of a complex balancing act. This balancing act does not follow a moral line, but a systemic one.

It does not ask what is right or wrong, but what is viable. Those who understand this logic stop seeing recommendations as a reflection of their own performance. They recognize them as an expression of a platform that regulates itself. This realization is sobering, but it is necessary. Because only those who understand why limitations exist can learn to deal with them. This section makes it clear that recommendations today have less to do with discovery and more to do with control. They are part of a larger mechanism that does not distribute attention, but shapes it. And it is precisely this shaping that creators sense, even if they have long been unable to name it. Chapter two takes this idea further. The next section reveals how this new logic specifically affects content. Not abstractly, but tangibly. Where creators notice that interest is no longer encouraged, but limited.

When interest is no longer encouraged, but limited

Interest has long been considered the driving force behind the platform. What generated attention was passed on. What aroused curiosity was reinforced. What captivated people was allowed to grow. This principle was so fundamental that it was hardly ever questioned. Interest seemed to be the natural ally of reach. But it is precisely this relationship that has shifted. Not openly, not declaratively, but functionally. Today, interest is no longer primarily encouraged. It is regulated. This regulation begins where interest loses its innocence. Interest is not neutral. It is an activator.

It directs attention, shapes expectations, influences decisions. The stronger the interest, the greater its influence. And influence is systemically delicate. Platforms that direct attention bear responsibility for the dynamics they trigger. This responsibility is not meant morally. It is structural. A system that generates too much interest at once destabilizes itself. YouTube has learned that interest is not an infinitely scalable commodity. It exhausts users. It overwhelms perception. It creates emotional peaks that lead to wear and tear in the long run. People who are constantly stimulated lose sensitivity. They switch off, become indifferent, or leave the platform.

This is precisely where the turning point lies. Interest had to be limited in order to maintain usage. This limitation is subtle. It does not manifest itself in making content uninteresting. It manifests itself in dosing interest. A user no longer gets everything that could captivate them to the maximum, but rather what keeps them in a stable state. This state is neither euphoric nor bored. It is balanced. From the system's point of view, this is the ideal user state. For creators, this logic is difficult to understand. They invest energy, creativity, and intelligence to generate interest. They build suspense, develop narratives, and condense content. And just when interest becomes strong, dissemination begins to stall. This paradox creates confusion because it contradicts the learned model of success. Interest is no longer seen as a positive reinforcement, but as a variable that needs to be controlled.

Content that attracts too much attention is treated with caution. Not because it is bad, but because it could throw users off balance. This balance is not individual, but collective. It affects not one user, but millions at the same time. The system therefore evaluates not only whether content is interesting, but how it generates interest. Is the interest calm or agitating? Is it short-lived or lasting? Does it lead to calm immersion or impulsive consumption? Content that generates impulsive interest is treated differently than content that leads to reflective engagement. Neither form is prohibited, but they are distributed differently. This differentiation is new.

In the past, attention was considered attention. Today, a distinction is made between different qualities of attention. This distinction is difficult to grasp algorithmically, but it is effective. It is reflected in the way content is recommended, how long it is tested, and how widely it is distributed. Interest is no longer simply passed on, but filtered. Many creators sense this filtering without being able to name it. They notice that videos that are highly captivating do not automatically grow. They see that content with high engagement remains in small groups. They experience that interest no longer leads to reach, but to stabilization at a certain level. These experiences are no coincidence. They are an expression of a platform that has learned to handle interest with care. This caution is also culturally conditioned. Societies have become more sensitive to overstimulation, emotional escalation, and the attention economy. Platforms respond to this sensitivity, not out of idealism, but out of adaptation. They must remain compatible with advertisers, regulatory authorities, and social expectations. Interest that polarizes or overwhelms too much is problematic in this context. YouTube therefore limits interest not selectively, but structurally. It shifts weights. It favors content that can be used continuously over content that generates intense peaks. It rewards reliability over excitement. This shift is not obvious, but it is effective. It changes what becomes visible. For creators, this creates a new conflict. They want to make content that people are really interested in. But genuine interest is rarely harmless. It demands attention. It demands engagement. It sometimes demands change.

It is precisely these demands that the system tries to dampen. Not to suppress them, but to control them. Interest thus becomes a double-edged sword. Too little interest leads to invisibility. Too much interest leads to limitation. In between lies a narrow corridor where content can have an impact without being considered destabilizing. This corridor is not static. It shifts. It depends on the topic, the context, the timing. And that is precisely why it is difficult to navigate. Many creators try to intuitively find this corridor. They adjust tone, depth, tempo. They sense that certain content is better received than others. This intuitive process is no coincidence. It is an adaptation to a system that no longer maximizes interest, but regulates it. But without understanding, this adaptation remains uncertain. It remains reactive. This section makes it clear that interest is no longer a guarantee of reach. It is a variable that is controlled. This realization is uncomfortable because it calls into question a central promise of the platform. But it is necessary in order to understand the behavior of the system. Interest has not disappeared. It has shifted. It is no longer collected, but distributed. No longer amplified, but dosed. Those who understand this stop wondering why strong content does not explode. They begin to realize that explosions are no longer the goal. Chapter two thus approaches its core. The platform has realigned itself. Recommendations follow a different logic. Change remained invisible for a long time. And interest is no longer promoted, but limited. The next section reveals the strategic consequences this has for creators. Not theoretically, but practically. It becomes clear how one can survive in a regulated system without giving up one's substance.

Why visibility is now given and no longer earned

Visibility was long linked to performance. This link was never perfect, but it was noticeable. Those who improved, who learned, who refined their content, could assume that this improvement would eventually be reflected externally. Visibility appeared to be the result of an implicit contract. Effort in exchange for reach. Quality in exchange for attention. This contract no longer exists in this form. Not because it was broken, but because the conditions under which it made sense have disappeared. Today, YouTube is a system that no longer understands visibility as a direct response to performance, but as a resource that must be distributed. This resource is limited, not technically, but functionally. Attention cannot grow indefinitely without destroying its own foundation. That is why it is managed today. And management follows different principles than reward. Earning implies fairness. It implies a linear relationship between effort and result. Systems that manage do not work with fairness, but with priorities. They do not ask who deserves something, but what is viable at a given moment. Visibility thus becomes a variable quantity. It is no longer the reward for good work, but the result of a weighing of factors. This weighing is complex.

It takes into account not only content, but contexts. Not only creators, but user states. Not only quality, but stability. In such a system, performance loses its direct translatability. Good content is necessary, but it is not sufficient. It is the ticket, not the guarantee. Many creators experience this change as an affront.

They have invested, learned, developed. They have done everything that used to work. And yet visibility remains elusive. This experience is painful because it affects their self-image. One would like to believe that effort counts. But visibility no longer follows this principle today. It follows the logic of allocation. Allocation is not an arbitrary act. It is the result of control. YouTube does not consciously decide on individual creators. It controls probabilities. It opens and closes distribution channels depending on how they affect the overall system. Visibility is increased where it has a stabilizing effect and limited where it has the potential to destabilize. This logic explains why visibility often seems uneven today. Why some content grows seemingly effortlessly, while other content stagnates despite its high quality. This inequality is not an expression of injustice, but of system priorities. Systems prioritize according to functional criteria, not moral ones. Another aspect of this allocation logic is temporal decoupling. Visibility no longer follows performance immediately. It can occur with a delay.

Content is archived, observed, and revisited later. Success is no longer decided in the moment, but over time. This delay makes orientation difficult. Creators no longer know where they stand. They work without clear feedback. But it is precisely this working without immediate reward that is part of the new selection process. Those who only work when visibility follows will fail in this system. Those who can work without being seen immediately have a chance. This shift is not cynical. It is a consequence of the fact that visibility is a strategic resource today. It is no longer distributed to motivate, but to stabilize. Visibility is therefore often granted today where it does not create surprises. Where content fits into familiar patterns. Where the effect remains predictable. This predictability is not synonymous with mediocrity, but it favors it. Mediocrity is predictable. It does not irritate. It does not challenge. It integrates well. This does not mean that exceptional content cannot gain visibility. It means that it must fit into a structure that makes its impact legible. Visibility is no longer enforced by excellence, but enabled by compatibility. This compatibility is not a betrayal of quality, but it does require translation. Many creators initially reject this insight. They perceive it as a devaluation of their work.

But in truth, it only shifts the focus. Away from the question of how to earn visibility, toward the question of how to enable it. This shift is subtle, but it changes the attitude. You no longer work to be rewarded, but to remain connected. Connectivity is the key concept. Content can be deep, complex, and sophisticated as long as it is presented in a form that the system can classify. This classification is not based on content, but on structure. It concerns rhythm, predictability, contextualization. Those who understand these levels can enable visibility without compromising themselves. Understanding visibility as an award is a relief. It relieves the creator of the illusion of being able to control everything. It ends self-accusation. It explains why good work sometimes remains invisible and why mediocre work can be visible. This explanation is uncomfortable, but it is honest. In a reward-based system, the concept of success also changes. Success is no longer about getting as much attention as possible, but about getting the right kind of attention.

Attention that lasts. That does not escalate. That does not overwhelm. This form of attention is less spectacular, but it is more sustainable. YouTube 2026 prefers sustainability over intensity. This is not an aesthetic judgment, but a functional one. Sustainable use keeps the platform running. Intense peaks endanger it. Visibility is therefore not awarded where it is most loudly demanded, but where it is sustainable in the long term. For creators, this means a new responsibility. Not in a moral sense, but in a strategic one. They have to decide what kind of visibility they want. Short-term explosions or long-term presence. Broad attention or stable resonance. These decisions are no longer dictated by the system. They lie with the creator. Chapter two ends at this point because this is where the core of the quiet realignment becomes visible. YouTube has evolved from a performance-oriented amplifier to a regulatory distributor. Visibility is no longer a reward, but an allocation. Those who understand this stop wondering. They begin to think differently. This different way of thinking is the prerequisite for everything else. Chapter three will show how this new logic is specifically reflected in the metrics. Why clicks, watch time, and frequency have lost their old power. And why the algorithm today measures something completely different from what creators have learned to optimize.

Notes:

Notes:

Chapter 3: When the algorithm stops thinking in terms of clicks

Why clicks have lost their significance

Clicks were long the most visible sign of success. They were at the beginning of every metric, every analysis, every optimization. A click meant interest. It meant a decision. It meant attention. Those who had a lot of clicks were considered relevant. Those who had few had to improve. This logic was simple, intuitive, and sufficient for a long time. But it no longer holds true. Clicks have not lost their significance because they have become unimportant, but because they have become too crude to measure what YouTube needs to control today. A click is a snapshot. It says something about curiosity, about impulse, about expectation. It says nothing about what happens next. At a time when growth was the primary goal, this information was sufficient. Clicks showed what people wanted to see. They helped spread content. They accelerated dynamics.

But in a system that prioritizes stability, clicks are not enough. They are loud but superficial. YouTube has learned that clicks are easy to generate. They can be manipulated, emotionalized, provoked. Thumbnails can arouse curiosity without delivering substance. Titles can create expectations that are not fulfilled. Clicks measure entry, not impact. And impact is what counts today. Not in the sense of opinion, but in the sense of behavioral change. A click can be the beginning of everything or the end of nothing. It can lead to deep engagement or immediate disappointment. For the system, this difference is crucial. Clicks alone say nothing about whether content is viable. They only say that it generates attention. However, attention without stability is problematic. It creates peaks, not loyalty. That's why the focus has shifted. Clicks haven't disappeared, but they have been devalued. They are an input signal, not a decision criterion. They open the door, but they no longer determine how far it opens. A video can have many clicks and still remain limited if the following effects are not right. Many creators have this experience without being able to classify it. The devaluation of clicks is part of a larger shift. YouTube no longer measures what people click on, but how they behave after clicking.

Do they remain calm or do they become restless? Do they stay on the platform or do they jump off? Do they delve deeper or do they scroll on? These subtle differences are what determine visibility. Clicks are only the trigger, not the benchmark. This change has profound consequences for content logic. Content that relies heavily on click optimization loses its effectiveness in the long run. It generates attention, but not stability. It attracts people, but it doesn't keep them in a state that the system prefers. That doesn't mean that excitement or curiosity are undesirable. It means that they need to be embedded. Many creators still cling to the old click logic because it is visible. Clicks can be counted. They can be compared. They give a feeling of control. But this control has become illusory.

Clicks are now a necessary but not sufficient factor. They no longer determine growth, but only whether content is even reviewed. YouTube now uses clicks as a filter rather than an amplifier. They show whether content could be relevant in principle. Everything else is decided later. In observation phases. In user paths. In behavior patterns. These processes are invisible, but they are effective. They elude classic creator analysis because they are not directly accessible. The result is a decoupling of effort and outcome. Creators optimize titles and thumbnails, see high click counts, and wonder why their reach remains limited. This discrepancy is not a mistake. It is a clue. An indication that clicks no longer measure what they used to measure. Clicks were a proxy for interest. Today, they are a proxy for impulse. Interest, on the other hand, is defined differently. It manifests itself in dwell time, but not in the traditional sense. It manifests itself in follow-up usage, in return visits, in consistency. These signals are quieter, but more meaningful. They don't show what people want, but how they stay. Understanding why clicks have lost their significance is the first step in comprehending the new metrics landscape. It explains why old optimization strategies no longer work. Why provocation no longer automatically scales. Why attention alone is not enough. This section therefore marks another departure. A departure from the idea that visibility can be enforced through attention. Today, visibility is created through compatibility. Clicks are only the beginning. Not the goal. Chapter three will continue this line of thought. The next section is about watch time. The metric that has long been considered the supreme discipline. And which today also plays a different role than most people believe.

Why watch time is no longer what it used to be

Watch time was long considered the most reliable currency on YouTube. It was deeper than clicks, more honest than likes, more stable than comments. Those who generated watch time were considered relevant. Those who kept people watching for a long time were rewarded. This logic was understandable because it promised proximity to actual usage. Time is limited. Those who get time must be doing something right. But even this metric has changed its role. Not because it has lost its significance, but because it has become too one-dimensional to reflect what YouTube needs to regulate today. Watch time measures duration, but not the quality of that duration. It tells you how long a video runs, not what happens to people during that time. It does not distinguish between passive consumption and active processing. It does not recognize whether someone is watching out of interest, habit, fatigue, or emotional dependence. In the early stages of the platform, this vagueness was sufficient. Today, it is problematic. Because time alone is no longer a reliable indicator of stable usage. YouTube has learned that high watch time does not automatically mean healthy usage. On the contrary. Content with extremely high watch time can cause overstimulation. It can draw users into states from which they find it difficult to escape. It can promote emotional dependence or cause mental exhaustion. These effects are not visible in the metric itself, but they are noticeable in subsequent behavior. And it is precisely this subsequent behavior that counts today. Watch time has long been an amplifier. Today, it is a raw signal. It shows that content is engaging, but it says nothing about whether this engagement is systemically desirable.

A video can keep people engaged for a long time and still be problematic if it leads to strong emotional swings or if it binds users into usage loops that are unstable in the long term. The system must recognize and regulate these effects. Watch time alone is not enough for this. That is why watch time is contextualized today. It is not viewed in isolation, but in relation to other factors. How does the user behave after watching the video? Do they remain calm or do they become restless? Do they switch to similar content in a controlled manner or do they jump around in an uncoordinated way? Do they leave the platform or do they remain in a stable usage pattern? These questions are crucial. Watch time is only part of the answer. Many creators continue to optimize for maximum watch time because they have learned that this metric is crucial. They extend videos, build in cliffhangers, and artificially maintain suspense. This may work in the short term. In the long term, however, it produces effects that the system no longer rewards. Content that is too engaging is treated with caution. Not because engagement is bad, but because it needs to be dosed. This marks another break with old success logic. In the past, the longer someone watched, the better. Today, the more stable someone remains afterwards, the more valuable they are. Stability is the new goal.

Watch time is evaluated based on whether it contributes to stable usage or more intense usage. Intense usage is risky. It creates peaks and valleys. It leads to fatigue. It increases the likelihood of abandonment. That's why YouTube now measures not only how long someone watches, but also how consistently. Consistency is an underestimated factor. It shows whether a user remains in a balanced state. Content that generates consistent attention is systemically more valuable than content that elicits extreme reactions. This consistency cannot be directly gleaned from watch time. It arises from patterns. Watch time is thus losing its former power. It is no longer the decisive lever for growth, but rather part of a more complex evaluation. A video with high watch time can stagnate if the follow-up effects are not right. A video with moderate watch time can grow if it contributes to stable usage paths.

This reversal is difficult for many creators to accept because it calls their previous work into question. The new role of watch time explains why in-depth content is often treated paradoxically. It keeps people engaged for a long time because it is complex. But it is precisely this complexity that can challenge users emotionally. It can trigger thought processes that do not immediately lead to further consumption behavior. Users take breaks, reflect, and may or may not come back later. This behavior is more difficult for the system to integrate than continuous viewing. That's why such content is often not scaled, even though its watch time is excellent. It doesn't fit into the ideal image of a stable usage chain. It interrupts flows instead of extending them. These interruptions are valuable to humans, but costly to the system. In this context, watch time is no longer seen as a success, but as a risk. YouTube has begun to differentiate watch time qualitatively without communicating this openly. It implicitly distinguishes between watch time that calms and watch time that stirs. Between watch time that leads to more consumption and watch time that leads to inner movement.

This distinction is difficult to grasp algorithmically, but it is real. It is based on patterns, not individual cases. For creators, this means a fundamental change. Watch time is no longer a goal, but a byproduct. Those who only extend content to increase watch time are working on the surface. What matters is not how long someone watches, but how they watch. This quality of viewing is difficult to influence, but it can be shaped. It can be shaped by rhythm, clarity, and internal logic. Content that does not overwhelm people, but guides them, creates a different kind of watch time. It is not spectacular, but stable. It doesn't hold on, but accompanies. This form of accompaniment is systemically desirable because it keeps users in a balanced state. Understanding why watch time is no longer what it used to be is central for creators from 2026 onwards. It explains why old strategies no longer work. Why extension does not automatically mean growth. Why depth is not automatically rewarded. Watch time has not disappeared. It has changed its role.

Today, it is one indicator among many, no longer king. It is interpreted, not added up. It is weighted, not set as absolute. Those who understand this stop chasing watch time. They begin to shape impact. This brings us to another key point. Clicks are losing their power. Watch time is losing its supremacy. The next section reveals why upload frequency and consistency are no longer what they used to be. And why today's algorithm no longer responds to activity, but to patterns.

Why activity and upload frequency have lost their controlling effect

For years, activity was considered a virtue. Regular uploading was not only recommended, but morally charged. Those who delivered consistently demonstrated seriousness. Those who took breaks risked being forgotten. Upload frequency became a discipline, consistency a creed. This logic was not accidental. In a phase where growth was supported by volume, it worked. More content meant more data. More data meant faster optimization. But that phase is over. Activity alone no longer controls anything. Upload frequency was a proxy. It stood for reliability, for commitment, for presence. But it said nothing about how content works. It only said that it exists. In a system that needs to stabilize, existence is not enough. Activity without effect is noise. And noise is what is regulated.

YouTube 2026 no longer evaluates how often something appears, but how consistent its effect is. Consistency is not the same as frequency. Consistency describes patterns. It describes whether content remains consistent, whether it produces predictable effects, whether it fits into existing usage path logic. One channel may publish infrequently and still appear consistent. Another may post daily and still appear chaotic. The system favors the former. Many creators stick to the old frequency logic because it is tangible. It provides structure. It gives the feeling of being able to do something.

But this feeling is deceptive. Frequent posting no longer automatically increases visibility. On the contrary, it can reduce it if content appears too densely, cannot be processed sufficiently, or disrupts the balance of usage. YouTube today measures not activity, but reliability of impact. Reliability means that content elicits similar reactions. That it doesn't throw users off their familiar paths. That it doesn't escalate unpredictably. Upload frequency is irrelevant here. A single video can have more impact than ten. And that's exactly why it's evaluated more intensively. Another aspect is saturation. In a system with billions of videos, every new video is a burden. Not technically, but cognitively. Users cannot absorb an unlimited amount of new content. The system has to make a selection. Frequency no longer plays a role in this selection. The decisive factor is whether content appears necessary. Necessary in the sense of appropriate, not in the sense of important. Regularity has long been a sign of commitment. Today, it is often a sign of interchangeability. Those who produce constantly must simplify. Simplification increases predictability, but it reduces significance. The system recognizes this trade-off. It prefers stability over quantity. Stability comes from clarity, not frequency. Many creators experience this change as paradoxical. They post more and achieve less.

They remain active and yet are slowed down. This experience often leads to even more activity in the hope of winning back the algorithm. But this spiral exacerbates the problem. Activity without strategic impact only increases the noise. YouTube has begun to decouple activity. A channel is no longer rated better just because it is present. Presence is a given. It is no longer an advantage. The advantage lies in pattern stability. This means that breaks no longer automatically cause harm. They can even be helpful if they intensify the effect. Content is given space to unfold. Users are given time to process it. This decoupling explains why some channels grow with few, well-placed videos, while others stagnate despite daily uploads. Growth does not come from frequency, but from fit. Fit between content, user state, and system goal. Upload frequency is only a marginal condition for this. The loss of control over activity also has a psychological dimension. Creators lose a clear recipe for action. They can no longer simply do more to get more. This powerlessness is uncomfortable. It forces reflection. It forces them to define impact not by diligence, but by design. Design means understanding content as events, not as commodities. Every video is an intervention in a system. It generates reactions.

These reactions must be integrable. Those who understand this no longer work against the platform, but within its logic. They use activity not as a means of pressure, but as a targeted impulse. Understanding why activity and upload frequency have lost their control effect dispels another myth. The myth that more is always better. In a stability-oriented system, the opposite is often the case. Less, but clearer, is more valuable than more, but more diffuse. In this third chapter, we show more and more clearly that the classic levers have lost their power. Clicks are devalued. Watch time is contextualized. Activity is relativized. In the next section, we will see what has replaced them. What patterns the algorithm actually reads today. And why these patterns are harder for creators to recognize, but more crucial than ever.

What the algorithm really reads today

The less visible the control becomes, the more it shifts to levels that are no longer intuitively comprehensible. That is exactly where the algorithm works today. Not on the surface of metrics, but in the spaces between them. It no longer reads individual signals, but constellations. Not numbers, but patterns. Not performance, but trends. If you want to understand why content grows or is limited, you have to learn to think in this new way. Today, the algorithm no longer reads whether a video performs well, but whether it behaves as expected. As expected does not mean boring, but integrable. Content can be interesting as long as it fits into familiar response paths. It can surprise as long as the surprise does not linger. It can touch as long as the touch does not lead to irritation. It is precisely these subtle differences that determine visibility.

What is read is not the video, but what it triggers. How do click intervals change? How do pauses change? How does the sequence of content consumed afterwards change? Does the user remain within a thematic framework or does he break out of it? Does he return or does he disappear? These movements are more meaningful to the system than any classic metric. The algorithm reads stability patterns. It recognizes whether content contributes to consistent usage or whether it generates fluctuations. Fluctuations are problematic because they are difficult to predict. They can trigger chain reactions. They can displace other content. They can cause emotional overload. These are all conditions that a stability-oriented system wants to avoid. These patterns do not arise in a video, but over time. The algorithm reads sequences. It observes how a channel develops. Whether topics remain consistent.

Whether the tone fluctuates. Whether the attitude is clear or changeable. A channel that changes significantly is read as uncertain, even if the content is high quality. Uncertainty is not a moral judgment. It is a statistical one. Many creators underestimate this temporal dimension. They view each video in isolation. Was it good? Was it successful? Was it better than the last one? But the system views the channel as a whole. It reads it as a progression, not as a collection. Individual outliers are less relevant than the overall dynamic. Growth occurs where this dynamic appears stable. The algorithm also reads emotional consistency. Not in terms of mood, but in terms of intensity. A channel that is calm today, stirring tomorrow, and provocative the day after tomorrow creates an unclear signature. This ambiguity makes classification difficult. A channel, on the other hand, that has a recognizable emotional base frequency is easier to integrate. It generates less variance. And variance is what is limited. What is read, therefore, is not content in the classic sense, but rather impact over time. This impact is difficult to manipulate because it cannot be directly controlled. You can change a title, optimize a thumbnail, extend a video. But you cannot force how people behave afterwards. That is precisely why these patterns are so valuable to the system. They are more robust than any single metric. The algorithm also reads deviations.

It recognizes when content falls outside the norm. Not to punish it, but to treat it with care. Deviations are tested, but not immediately scaled. They are played out in small doses, observed, and classified. Only when they prove to be integrable does the space for growth open up. This process takes time. And it is not transparent. This lack of transparency creates uncertainty. Creators don't know why a video remains limited. They only see the result, not the process. This uncertainty often leads to misinterpretations. People look for errors in the content, even though the problem lies in the pattern. They optimize individual elements, even though the whole is being read. What the algorithm really reads today is therefore not easily accessible. It requires a rethink. Away from the idea that you can tweak individual settings, towards the realization that you create an overall impression. This overall impression is created by consistency, clarity, and rhythmic stability. Rhythm is an underestimated factor. Not upload rhythm, but impact rhythm.

How often does a channel demand attention? How strongly? How intensely? A channel that constantly generates maximum intensity is perceived as stressful. A channel that rhythmically combines tension and relief appears more stable. This stability is attractive to the system. The algorithm also reads how content ages. Whether it remains relevant over time or quickly fizzles out. Content that has a lasting effect but does not generate escalation is valuable. It can be played again and again without creating new risks. This long-term stability is more important than short-term peaks. Many creators still work against this logic because they don't see it. They optimize for what is measurable and overlook what is readable. But what is read is what matters. Not today, not tomorrow, but over time. Growth is no longer a moment. It is a state. Chapter three thus approaches its core. Classic metrics are losing their power because they are too superficial. They are being replaced by patterns that are more difficult to grasp but more stable. The next section will clarify why exactly these patterns are so difficult for creators to consciously shape. And why many unconsciously do exactly what limits their reach.

Why creators unconsciously work against the new patterns

The greatest difficulty in dealing with the new algorithmic logic lies not in its complexity, but in its invisibility. People depend on feedback to adjust their behavior. When this feedback is missing or distorted, they fall back on old models. This is exactly what is currently happening on YouTube. Creators are not working against the algorithm because they ignore it, but because they interpret it based on outdated signals. They optimize where nothing is decided anymore, thereby unconsciously reinforcing the very patterns that limit their reach. The human impulse is understandable. When something no longer works, you increase your efforts. More energy, more presence, more intensity. This behavior makes sense in many areas of life. In a stability-oriented system, however, it is counterproductive. Intensification increases variance. Variance increases uncertainty. Uncertainty is regulated. This is precisely where the vicious circle arises that many creators experience without being able to name it. Unconscious counteraction usually begins when creators try to serve several logics at the same time. They want to remain relevant and grow at the same time.

They want depth and reach. They want development and stability. These goals are not fundamentally contradictory, but they require conscious design. Without this awareness, incoherence arises. Content sends mixed signals. The algorithm does not read a clear line, but an oscillating profile. Oscillation is difficult to integrate. It appears unstable. A common pattern is overcompensation. As reach declines, content becomes more emotional. Titles become more pointed. Thumbnails become louder. Topics become more extreme. In the short term, this can generate attention. In the long term, however, it increases the dispersion of the effect. The system recognizes this dispersion and responds with further restrictions. The creator interprets this as a sign that they need to apply even more pressure. The spiral intensifies. Another unconscious counter-pattern is fragmentation. Creators respond to stagnating numbers by trying out new formats, testing new topics, and addressing new target groups. These experiments are humanly understandable. They signal activity and a willingness to adapt. For the system, however, they create blurring. The channel loses readability.

Its effect becomes more diffuse. Growth becomes less likely. Even the attempt to do everything right often has a limiting effect. Creators consume advice, analyze trends, and adapt to best practices. They optimize titles, structure, and length. But these optimizations are usually based on visible models of success, not on the underlying patterns. They copy surfaces, not impact logic. The result is interchangeability. Interchangeability is predictable, but it is also saturated. The system does not favor it in the long term. A particularly subtle mechanism is the emotional self-regulation of creators. Declining reach creates uncertainty. Uncertainty influences tone. Content becomes more cautious, defensive, or, conversely, more aggressive. These emotional shifts are noticeable to viewers. They change the effect. The algorithm does not read this change as authenticity, but as instability. It reacts accordingly. Unconscious countermeasures are also evident in the handling of breaks.

Many creators fear pauses because they have learned that activity is important. They continue to produce, even if the content is not yet ready. This overproduction reduces density. Videos appear unfocused. The effect becomes flatter. The system reads declining clarity of effect and limits it. The cause is not recognized because it does not lie in the individual video, but in the rhythm. The core of all these patterns is the same. Creators try to force visibility, while the system grants visibility. Forcing creates pressure. Pressure creates variance. Variance is regulated. This dynamic is not intuitive because it contradicts the human understanding of performance. However, it is consistent within a system that prioritizes stability. Another aspect is the confusion between authenticity and spontaneity. Many creators believe that genuine content must be created unrestrainedly. That you should say what is on your mind. This attitude is valuable from a human perspective, but challenging from a systemic perspective. Spontaneous impact is difficult to classify.

It generates unpredictable reactions. Without structural embedding, it is interpreted as a risk. Authenticity without form loses readability. The system does not favor untruth. It favors structure. Structure makes impact integrable. Creators who work against structure often believe they are staying true to themselves. In reality, they make it difficult for the system to classify their content. The result is not rejection, but restraint. Reach remains limited, even though the content is honest. Many creators also work against the new patterns because they still understand success as an event. A video goes viral. A channel explodes. These images shape expectations. But today, success is a state of being. It manifests itself in consistent presence, stable impact, and slow opening. Those who continue to work toward events create peaks that cannot be sustained. Unconscious counteraction is therefore not a mistake on the part of individual creators. It is a collective delay in adaptation. The platform has changed faster than the mental model of the people who work on it. This delay creates friction.

Friction is experienced as personal failure, even though it is structural. The way out of this dynamic lies not in further optimization, but in a change of perspective. Creators must stop viewing the algorithm as an adversary or judge. It is a reader. It reads patterns. If you want to be read, you have to write, not shout. Writing means structure. It means rhythm. It means clarity about your own impact. Clarity is not a matter of content, but of form. You can say complex things clearly. You can unfold depth in a structured way. You can make development visible without appearing chaotic. These skills are not intuitive. They require awareness. And it is precisely this awareness that many lack because it was not necessary in the old logic. Understanding why creators unconsciously work against the new patterns is the conclusion of chapter three.

It shows that the loss of the old levers is not the problem. The problem is clinging to them. Those who recognize that clicks, watch time, frequency, and activity have lost their control function can stop overemphasizing them. They can begin to shape what is actually read. This shaping is more demanding, but it is more honest. It forces us to confront our own impact. It demands responsibility. Not to the system, but to our own actions. This responsibility is the price of long-term presence in a regulated space. This is where chapter three ends, because at this point a complete break has been made. The old tools have lost their power. The new ones are invisible. Those who do not recognize them struggle. Those who recognize them position themselves. Chapter four will continue this step. It shows why YouTube no longer promotes interest but limits it, and what psychological mechanisms are behind this decision.

Notes:

Notes:

Chapter 4: Why YouTube limits interest instead of promoting it

Why interest is now seen as a burden

Interest has long been the fuel of the platform. It was considered an unconditional value. Whatever interested people was allowed to grow. Whatever aroused curiosity was reinforced. This logic was based on an almost romantic idea of freedom. The best ideas prevail. The most exciting content finds its audience. Attention follows quality. This idea has not disappeared, but it has been gutted. Today, interest is no longer seen as a resource, but as a burden. And burdens must be regulated. The reason for this lies not in interest itself, but in its effect. Interest activates. It attracts attention, focuses it, holds it. This focusing is not neutral. It changes perception, mood, decision-making processes. The more intense the interest, the more it interferes with a person's inner dynamics. Platforms that address billions of people at the same time cannot allow these interventions indefinitely without causing side effects.

YouTube has learned in recent years that interest does not automatically lead to satisfaction. On the contrary. Strong interest can create overload. It can cause emotional peaks that cannot be integrated in the long term. Users then feel empty, exhausted, or irritable. They consume more, but they do not remain stable. This instability is problematic for a system that depends on long-term use. That is why the assessment of interest has shifted. The question is no longer whether something is interesting, but how it interests. Whether it calms or agitates. Whether it focuses or distracts. Whether it fits into existing usage patterns or breaks them. Interest that is too out of the ordinary is seen as a burden. Not because it is wrong, but because it is difficult to integrate. This new interpretation of interest explains why many highly attractive types of content are restricted. They attract people, but they change their state too much. It creates expectations that cannot be continuously fulfilled. It amplifies emotional fluctuations. All of this increases the systemic load. Platforms respond to this not with bans, but with dosage. Dosage is the central instrument of the new logic.

Interest is not suppressed, but distributed. It is portioned, stretched out over time, embedded in contexts. Content may fascinate, but it must not dominate. It may move, but it must not overwhelm. These subtle gradations are difficult to see, but they are effective. For creators, this shift is irritating. They have learned that interest is the key. They invest in dramaturgy, in storytelling, in building suspense. And it is precisely these efforts that lead to content being treated more cautiously. Not because it is poorly made, but because it triggers too much. This paradox is difficult to accept because it contradicts one's own craft. Interest is now seen as a burden because it binds attention. Bound attention is not available to other content. It narrows the space for perception. In a platform economy that has to simulate diversity, too strong a bond is problematic. It creates monocultures. It amplifies individual voices at the expense of others. Platforms have learned that such monocultures are unstable in the long term. That is why interest is no longer maximized, but distributed. Not everything that is of great interest becomes big. Not everything that captivates is scaled.

The system no longer asks how much interest something generates, but how well it fits into the overall landscape. This landscape is no longer an open market, but a regulated space. Another aspect is the predictability of interest. Strong interests are often unpredictable. They arise quickly, grow explosively, and collapse abruptly. Such dynamics are difficult to control. They create peaks that cannot be smoothed out. Platforms respond to this unpredictability with caution. They do not slow down interest, but rather its spread. This caution is not new, but it has become more consistent. In the past, explosive trends were tolerated because growth was more important. Today, they are embedded because stability is more important. This shift in priorities changes what becomes visible. Content that generates consistently moderate interest is preferred. Content that generates extreme interest is curtailed.

For creators, this means a new reality. Interest is no longer a guarantee of reach. It is a variable that is evaluated. It can help, but it can also hurt. This ambivalence makes planning difficult. You can no longer simply say, "This topic is interesting, so it will work." You have to ask what kind of interest it generates and how it fits into the system. Many creators feel this ambivalence without being able to name it. They experience that content with a strong response does not grow. They receive intense feedback, but no scaling. This divergence between response and reach is no coincidence. It is an expression of a platform that no longer uses interest as a growth engine, but treats it as a burden. Interest is therefore now placed more strongly in context. It is not viewed in isolation, but in the context of overall user behavior. Content that generates strong interest but then leads to abandonment is evaluated differently than content that generates moderate interest and keeps users in a stable state. This evaluation is not intuitive, but it is consistent. The idea that interest must be limited is difficult for many creators to accept because it contradicts their own drive.

Creatives want to move people. They want to fascinate. They want to trigger something. But it is precisely this effect that is being systematically regulated. Not to suppress creativity, but to keep the system viable. This tension is at the heart of chapter four. YouTube no longer promotes interest unconditionally, but conditionally. It no longer asks whether something is exciting, but whether it is manageable. This question is uncomfortable because it marks a boundary. But it is real. Those who recognize this boundary can work differently. They can shape interest in such a way that it has an effect without overloading. They can develop depth without escalating. They can create tension without building peaks that the system avoids. This form of design is challenging, but it is possible. Chapter four will show what this design looks like. Not as a guide, but as an understanding. Because only when it is clear why interest is seen as a burden today does it become understandable why the platform acts the way it does. And why creators who recognize this have a decisive advantage.

The psychology of platform stability

Stability is not a technical state, but a psychological one. Platforms do not exist independently of the people who use them. Every technical decision affects perception, emotion, and behavior. YouTube has understood that long-term use is not created by maximum stimulation, but by regulated experience. This realization marks a turning point. The focus is no longer on what interests people, but on what state they should be kept in. Platform stability means keeping users in an emotional balance. Not euphoric, not frustrated, not overwhelmed. A state of moderate activation is considered optimal. In this state, people consume regularly, make predictable decisions, and remain open to new content without being overwhelmed by it. This goal is not arbitrary. It is based on decades of research on attention economics and behavioral psychology. YouTube no longer works primarily with rewards, but with regulation. Regulation is more subtle than rewards. It does not work through clear reinforcement, but through framework conditions. Users should not feel particularly good or particularly bad. They should feel sufficiently stimulated to stay, but not so strongly that they tip over. This balance is fragile. And that is precisely why it is protected. In the early days of digital platforms, escalation was accepted. Attention was to be maximized. Strong emotions were considered a success. Anger, enthusiasm, fear, fascination. Anything that engaged users was reinforced. This phase has left its mark. Polarization, exhaustion, loss of trust. Platforms have responded to this, not out of moral insight, but out of self-preservation. The psychology of platform stability is based on the realization that extreme emotional states are not sustainable.

Users who are overstimulated burn out. They reduce their usage or turn away. Users who are understimulated get bored. They also turn away. The stable user is somewhere in between. And it is precisely this user state that is sought after today. Interest is therefore evaluated psychologically. Not according to how strong it is, but according to how it affects users. Interest that is too strong is dampened. Interest that is too weak is ignored. In between lies a range in which content is considered acceptable. This acceptability is not an aesthetic judgment. It is a psychological one. YouTube does not measure feelings directly. It measures behavior. But behavior is a reliable indicator of inner states. Fast scrolling, frequent switching, abrupt interruptions, long pauses. All these patterns tell a story. They show whether users are overwhelmed, bored, or balanced. These signals flow into the evaluation of content, even if they are never openly named. Platform stability also means avoiding extreme dependencies. Content that binds users too strongly is successful in the short term, but problematic in the long term.

It reduces diversity, increases pressure to perform, and reinforces emotional dependence. Platforms respond to this with cautious distribution. They limit reach not to punish, but to prevent dependence. This logic contradicts the classic creator ideal. Many want to bind. They want to build communities and accompany people over the long term. But from a systemic perspective, exclusive binding is tricky. It makes users less flexible. It makes balance more difficult. Platforms prefer loose binding over rigid loyalty. This preference is not ideological, but functional. The psychology of platform stability also explains why education, depth, and reflection are often limited. Not because they are undesirable, but because they lead users into internal processes that do not immediately result in further consumer behavior. People pause. They reflect. They take breaks. This is valuable for the individual. For the system, it is a break in the usage path. YouTube tries to minimize these breaks.

Not by prohibiting them, but by isolating them. Content that strongly encourages reflection is played in a targeted manner, but not en masse. It is allowed to exist, but it should not dominate the overall flow. This isolation is not a judgment on the content, but a protective measure for the system. Stability also means predictability. Users should feel safe. They should know what to expect. Surprises are allowed, but they must be embedded. A system that constantly surprises causes stress. Stress reduces long-term use. That's why surprises are dosed. They are allowed to happen, but they must not escalate. For creators, this presents a new challenge. They must learn to think psychologically about impact. Not in the sense of manipulation, but in the sense of responsibility. What states do their contents create? How intense are these states? How long do they last? These questions are complex, but they are crucial. Many creators underestimate the psychological dimension of their work. They think in terms of content, not states. But platforms think in terms of states. They don't ask what is being said, but what it triggers. Those who understand this can design their content to be effective without having a destabilizing effect. The psychology of platform stability is no secret. It is the logical consequence of a platform that has come of age. YouTube can no longer afford extremes. It has to balance, dampen, regulate. This necessity shapes the recommendation logic. It shapes what becomes visible. It shapes how creators are perceived. This section makes it clear that reach today is not only a technical issue, but also a psychological one. If you want reach, you have to be not only interesting, but also compatible. Compatible with users, with the system, with the cultural context. This compatibility can be shaped, but it requires awareness. Chapter four takes this idea further. The next section reveals why exactly this psychological logic leads to certain content being favored and other content being restricted. Not because of its subject matter, but because of its depth of impact.

Why certain content must be toned down in order to grow

The larger a platform becomes, the less it can afford to leave open what content does to people. YouTube has long since crossed this threshold. Today, content must not only inform, entertain, or inspire. Above all, it must do one thing. It must be calming. Not in the sense of boredom, but in the sense of inner regulation. Growth is linked to this state because only calming content is systemically sustainable. Reassurance does not mean passivity. It means emotional embedding. Content can be exciting as long as it does not destabilize. It can be moving as long as it does not upset. It can be irritating as long as it does not unsettle. These subtle differences determine whether content is scaled or not. Reassuring content does not cause fluctuations. It smooths transitions. It leads users back to familiar emotional zones. YouTube does not measure these effects consciously, but indirectly. It observes how people react after consumption. Do they remain in a similar emotional state? Do they feel oriented or lost? Do they continue consuming or do they stop? These behavior patterns are psychological markers.

They show whether content has a calming or destabilizing effect. And these markers influence distribution. Content that is calming is easier to scale because it does not trigger chain reactions. It does not change fundamental patterns of perception. It confirms more than it questions. That does not mean it has to be superficial. Even complex content can have a calming effect if it is structured, if it guides, if it conveys a sense of order. Order is a psychological calming factor. Disorder, on the other hand, is systemically problematic. Content that deliberately leaves things open, celebrates ambivalence, raises questions without providing answers, is valuable to humans but risky for algorithms. It creates inner movement. Movement leads to pauses, to pausing, to deviation from the consumption path. This deviation is difficult for the system to integrate. It is therefore limited. Many creators confuse reassurance with conformity. They believe that content must be made shallower in order to grow. But that is not the core issue. The core issue is structure. Reassurance comes from clarity, not simplification.

Content can be profound and still be reassuring if it does not leave the viewer feeling disoriented. Orientation is the key. YouTube prefers content that offers an inner conclusion. Not in the sense of definitive answers, but in the sense of psychological closure. Content that builds tension must also resolve it. Content that asks questions must offer a framework in which these questions can be held. Open endings are humanly exciting, but systemically difficult. This logic explains why much content with strong intellectual or emotional appeal remains limited. It leaves people in a state that cannot be immediately integrated. This state is valuable for personal development, but it disrupts the cycle of use. The system responds to this with caution. Reassuring content, on the other hand, stabilizes the cycle. It allows for continued consumption without overwhelming the user. It keeps users in a state that is neither too passive nor too active. This state is optimal for long-term use.

That is why such content is preferred. Not because of content evaluation, but because of psychological necessity. This insight is central for creators. Growth no longer depends on how strongly you charge something, but how well you embed it. A powerful idea needs a calm setting. A provocative thesis needs a clear structure. An emotional story needs a secure conclusion. These elements are not questions of style. They are growth factors. Many creators unconsciously work against this logic because they believe that openness and irritation are signs of depth. They are. But without embedding, they are seen as a risk. The system is not against depth. It is against destabilization. Those who design depth in such a way that it calms rather than overwhelms can grow without betraying themselves. Reassurance also means recognizability. Content that is familiar in tone, rhythm, and structure creates security.

Security is a prerequisite for openness. Users who feel secure are more willing to take in new things. This security is not trivial. It arises from consistent design. YouTube therefore scales content that appears familiar, even if it contains new ideas. Familiarity reduces risk. It makes impact predictable. Predictability is the basis for control. Control enables growth. This chain is not intuitive, but it is effective. Understanding why certain content must be reassuring in order to grow shifts the focus from volume to structure. It explains why many brilliant pieces of content remain limited, while seemingly unspectacular ones grow. It also explains why some creators are successful despite their depth. They have learned to package depth in calmness. This section marks an important turning point. Growth no longer comes from maximum impact, but from regulated impact. Not through escalation, but through integration. This realization is uncomfortable, but it opens up new possibilities. Chapter four will continue this thought. The next section is about why YouTube is increasingly avoiding strong emotions and what cultural and economic reasons are behind this development.

Why strong emotions are increasingly being avoided

Strong emotions have long been considered the surest way to attract attention. Anger, enthusiasm, fear, outrage, euphoria. Anything that threw people off balance kept them hooked. This dynamic was not a side effect, but a driving force behind the early platform economy. Attention followed intensity. Reach followed reaction. But it is precisely this logic that has proven problematic in the long term. YouTube avoids strong emotions today not out of moral caution, but out of structural self-protection. Emotions are amplifiers. They accelerate perception, shorten reaction times, and increase engagement. But they come at a price. Strong emotions are exhausting. They consume mental resources. Users who are permanently emotionally highly activated become unstable.

They react more impulsively, jump faster, and abruptly stop using the platform. For a system that relies on continuous, predictable use, this is a risk. YouTube has recognized that emotional escalation is not a sustainable business model. It generates short-term peaks, but long-term wear and tear. Users who are constantly challenged emotionally develop defense mechanisms. They become cynical, indifferent, or avoid certain content altogether. These reactions reduce long-term use. Platforms respond to this not with bans, but with reweighting. Strong emotions are not excluded, but they are deprioritized. Content that regularly generates strong emotional swings is distributed more cautiously. Not because it is wrong, but because it jeopardizes the emotional balance of users. YouTube tries to smooth out emotional curves. It favors content that generates moderate activation and then reduces it again. This smoothing is a central element of the new platform logic. Emotions are allowed to arise, but they must be regulatable. Content that generates open outrage, sustained fear, or extreme enthusiasm is difficult to integrate. It leads to aftereffects that cannot simply be transferred to the next piece of content. Users get stuck, but not in the sense of stable use, but in the sense of emotional fixation.

Fixation is systemically problematic. It reduces flexibility. Users who are emotionally fixed consume less diversely. They react more strongly to certain triggers and less strongly to others. This polarization makes it difficult to achieve balance. Platforms have learned that such fixations undermine their ability to control in the long term. YouTube therefore avoids strong emotions not selectively, but structurally. It changes which content can be easily scaled. It prefers emotional sequences that can be closed. Tension may arise, but it must be resolved. Concern may be present, but it must be classified. Enthusiasm may arise, but it must not tip over. This development is particularly irritating for creators because emotions are a central means of expression. They lend content power, authenticity, and urgency. Many creators have learned to consciously use their emotionality to reach people. And it is precisely this ability that is now being systematically limited. Not because it is undesirable, but because it is too effective. Strong emotions generate unpredictable follow-up reactions. An emotionally charged video can cause users to immerse themselves in similar content for hours or, conversely, to abruptly switch off. Both reactions are problematic. They destabilize usage patterns. The system responds by including such content less frequently in broad recommendations. This restraint is often misunderstood as censorship.

But it is not an evaluation of content. It is not about what is said, but how it affects people. A factual video on a controversial topic can grow if it is emotionally regulated. An emotional video on a harmless topic can be limited if it generates strong reactions. The emotional impact is more decisive than the topic. YouTube also responds to external expectations in this way. Advertisers, regulatory authorities, social discourse. A platform that is perceived as emotionally escalating loses trust. However, trust is a prerequisite for long-term monetization. Stable emotions are more economically valuable than intense ones. This economic dimension is rarely addressed openly, but it is central. YouTube is not a cultural project, but an economic system. Economic systems favor stability. They avoid risks. Emotional escalation is a risk. It can trigger scandals, provoke political reactions, and lead to regulatory intervention. All of this is to be avoided. For creators, this means a new boundary.

Not everything that is emotionally powerful is allowed to grow. Emotions must be guided. They must be embedded in structure, context, and resolution. Content that opens up emotions must also offer a way to close them again. This ability is increasingly rewarded. Many creators experience this change as a loss of freedom. They feel restricted in their expression. But this restriction is not absolute. It merely requires a different form. Emotions are allowed to be there, but they must not be left to their own devices. They must be shaped. Shaping means responsibility. Not in a moral sense, but in a systemic sense. Those who generate emotions generate impact. Impact has consequences. YouTube responds to these consequences by favoring content that is emotionally controllable. This preference is not visible, but it is effective. Understanding why strong emotions are increasingly avoided helps creators better classify their own impact. It explains why some passionate content remains limited. It also explains why calm, seemingly less intense content can grow. It is more emotionally compatible. This section leads to a key insight. Growth today does not come from maximum emotional activation, but from emotional balance. This balance is not a loss of depth. It is a different form of depth. One that works not through overwhelm, but through embedding. The next section reveals why YouTube pursues this emotional regulation not only for psychological reasons, but also for economic reasons. And why these reasons are crucial for creators to truly understand the platform.

Why economic security is more important than maximum attention

At the end of every platform logic is not an ideology, but a calculation. YouTube is not a neutral space for cultural exchange, but an economic system with clear dependencies. These dependencies determine what is promoted and what is not. Attention was long the central commodity because it promised growth. Today, attention is only valuable if it is economically secure. And this is precisely the deepest reason why interest, emotion, and impact are limited. Economic security means predictability. Advertising revenue must be calculable. User behavior must remain stable. Brands must be able to operate in an environment that does not burden them with reputational risks. YouTube has a responsibility to create this environment. Not explicitly, not morally, but functionally. A platform that becomes too turbulent loses advertising customers. And without advertising customers, it loses its foundation. Maximum attention is ambivalent from an economic perspective. It can increase revenue in the short term, but create risks in the long term.

Attention that is highly emotional attracts controversy. Controversy creates uncertainty. Uncertainty deters advertising customers. That is why attention is no longer maximized today, but qualified. It is evaluated according to whether it fits into a stable advertising environment. This qualification is invisible, but consistent. Content that elicits strong reactions is more difficult to monetize. Not because it is illegal or inappropriate, but because it is difficult to predict. Brands want to know the context in which they appear. They want security. This security is easier to guarantee with moderate, well-embedded content than with polarizing or emotionally charged content. YouTube therefore no longer optimizes for maximum dwell time or maximum interaction, but for economic viability. Content is viable if it remains continuously monetizable without creating regulatory, social, or brand-related risks. This definition of success differs fundamentally from the creative definition of many creators. Creators think in terms of impact.

Platforms think in terms of risk. These two perspectives are not congruent. Impact can be valuable, but it can also be expensive. It can focus attention, but it can also trigger conflicts. YouTube responds to this ambivalence by embedding impact. Not to prevent it, but to make it calculable. Economic security also means not losing users. Users who feel emotionally overwhelmed are less loyal. They pause, reduce usage, or turn away. This exodus is gradual, but it is measurable. Platforms respond to such signals early, before they become visible. Limiting intense content is a preventive measure. It protects the platform from long-term loss of usage. This protective logic explains why content that is highly polarizing or emotional is often not scaled, even if it generates high interaction. Interaction alone is no longer a sign of quality. It must be embedded in an environment that remains economically stable. Content that could jeopardize this environment is treated with caution. Many creators find this logic cold. They feel reduced to their monetizability. But this reduction is not personal. It is structural. YouTube cannot act differently without jeopardizing its own existence. A platform of this size must prioritize economic security, even if it limits creative potential. This realization is uncomfortable, but it is clarifying. It ends the illusion that reach is purely a judgment of quality. Reach is an economic signal. It shows that content not only works, but is also safe. Safe for users. Safe for brands.

Safe for the system. Economic security has therefore become more important than maximum attention. Attention is volatile. Security is stable. In a mature platform economy, stability wins. This priority shapes every recommendation, every limitation, every dampening. It is the invisible framework within which everything moves. For creators, this means a new reality. If you want to grow, you not only have to be interesting, but also economically integrable. This does not mean selling out or watering down content. It means designing impact in such a way that it does not create unnecessary risks. This design is challenging, but it is possible. Many creators fail not because of a lack of quality, but because of a lack of translation. They create impact, but they do not translate it into a form that the system can support. This translation is not censorship of content.

It is a formal adaptation. Those who master it can maintain depth and still grow. Chapter four ends here because at this point the logic becomes completely visible. Interest is limited, emotions are regulated, not out of arbitrariness, but out of economic necessity. YouTube stabilizes itself because it has to. And creators who understand this can stop fighting against this stabilization. In chapter five, we will continue these thoughts. It shows why platforms become particularly cautious when creators begin to develop real personalities. And why, paradoxically, this very strength becomes a risk.

Notes:

Notes:

Chapter 5: The platform's fear of real personalities

Why real personalities become systemically unpredictable

Platforms love profiles, but they fear personalities. This difference is subtle, but crucial. A profile is predictable. It stands for a theme, a style, an expectation. It can be classified, clustered, passed on. A personality, on the other hand, is alive. It develops. It contradicts itself. It changes its perspective. It is precisely this liveliness that is humanly attractive but systemically risky. YouTube does not address this risk openly, but indirectly, by carefully limiting the spread of real personalities. Real personalities defy simple attributions. They are not only content carriers, but also meaning carriers. People follow them not because of a topic, but because of an attitude. This attitude has an impact beyond videos. It shapes perception, trust, and orientation. This is valuable for the audience. For the system, it is problematic. Because meaning is difficult to control. It cannot be standardized. It scales unevenly. A creator with a clear personality creates loyalty. This loyalty is deeper than interest. It is not limited to individual content, but extends across channels.

Users begin to filter content through the person. They listen differently. They react differently. They make decisions differently. This shift changes usage patterns. And it is precisely this change that makes platforms cautious. Profiles can be replaced. Personalities cannot. A profile can be copied, a format reproduced, a style adapted. Personalities, on the other hand, create uniqueness. Uniqueness is not scalable in the traditional sense. It creates peaks, but not even distribution. Platforms that need to create balance respond to such peaks with regulation. YouTube therefore favors channels that function as profiles. A clearly defined theme. A consistent tone. An predictable attitude. These elements create reliability. Reliability enables prediction. Prediction enables control. Personalities, on the other hand, bring movement to this structure. They evolve, react to events, change their language. This dynamic is humanly comprehensible, but algorithmically difficult to integrate. Many creators experience this effect as soon as they begin to really show themselves. As soon as content no longer just informs or entertains, but carries a personal perspective, the system's response changes. Reach becomes more cautious. Growth slows down. Not because the content gets worse, but because it becomes more individual. Individuality increases variance.

Variance increases risk. Real personalities also generate loyalty. Loyalty is desirable for creators, but ambivalent for platforms. Loyalty reduces willingness to switch. Users who are strongly attached to one person consume less diversely. They stray from familiar paths. For the system, however, diversity is a factor of stability. It distributes attention. It prevents dependencies. That is why exclusive attachments are treated with caution. This caution is not expressed as a prohibition, but as a limitation. Personalities are allowed to exist, but they must not dominate. They are allowed to have an impact, but they should not dominate the space. This logic is not explicit, but it is noticeable. Creators with strong personal charisma often achieve an intense but limited reach. Their impact is deep but not broad. Another aspect is the unpredictability of genuine personalities. They respond to feedback.

They change their minds. They talk about things that move them. This spontaneity is humanly attractive, but systemically risky. Platforms prefer channels whose content can be explained by the format, not by a person's inner movement. YouTube has learned that personalities have influence. Influence is not neutral. It can strengthen trust, but it can also create expectations that are difficult to control. People orient themselves toward personalities, not just information. This orientation can have positive effects, but it can also exacerbate conflicts. Platforms respond to this influence with restraint. For creators, this realization is painful. They have learned that authenticity is a value. That you should grow by showing yourself. And that's true. Authenticity works. But it doesn't always work in terms of reach. It works in terms of meaning. Meaning is not the primary goal of a stability-oriented system.

Understanding why real personalities become systemically unpredictable is another step in the shift in perspective. It explains why some of the most influential creators are not the biggest. It explains why depth and personality often go hand in hand with limited reach. And it explains why conformity is rewarded in the short term but empties out in the long term. This section marks the beginning of a central theme of the book: the tension between personality and platform, between human development and systemic stability. This tension cannot be resolved, but it can be shaped. How this shaping can look without losing personality becomes clear in the course of chapter five. Because YouTube does not fear people. It fears uncontrollability. And real personalities are exactly that.

Why strong creators are paradoxically held back

Strength is not a neutral state. It changes relationships. It shifts balances. It creates dependencies. In human systems, strength is often admired, but in technical systems, it is viewed with suspicion. This is precisely where the paradox that many successful creators experience arises. The stronger they become, the more cautiously the platform reacts. Not despite their strength, but because of it. A strong creator is not simply someone with reach. Strength arises where impact goes beyond individual content. Where people don't just consume, but follow. Where trust is built. Where statements carry weight. This form of strength is qualitative, not quantitative.

It is not only reflected in numbers, but also in the way content is received. Comments become more personal. Feedback becomes more intense. Expectations become clearer. It is precisely this intensity that the system begins to regulate. YouTube does not evaluate strength as success, but as influence. Influence is ambivalent. It can stabilize, but it can also shift. A strong creator can set trends, shape discourse, and influence moods. This ability is valuable to humans, but systemically sensitive. Platforms are designed to distribute influence, not concentrate it. Concentration creates power. Power creates responsibility. Responsibility creates risk. That is why, paradoxically, strong creators are slowed down. Not openly, not punitively, but subtly. Growth slows down. Recommendations become more selective. Reach stabilizes at a plateau.

This plateau is no coincidence. It is a point of equilibrium where influence still seems acceptable. Beyond that, caution prevails. This caution is not personal. It is not directed against content or opinions. It is directed against the dynamics of influence. Platforms have learned that too much influence on individual actors makes the system vulnerable. Scandals, shifts in opinion, personal crises. All of this can have massive repercussions when influence is concentrated. Decentralization is therefore a key principle of stability. Strong creators are difficult to decentralize. Their impact cannot simply be distributed to others. They are not interchangeable. This is precisely what makes them valuable to their audience and risky for the platform. YouTube responds to this by not allowing their reach to grow indefinitely. It lets them have an impact, but prevents them from becoming dominant. Many creators interpret this limitation as unfair. They have done everything right. They have delivered quality. They have built trust. And yet they remain below their potential. But this interpretation falls short. The limitation is not an assessment of performance, but a regulation of impact. Another aspect is the dynamics of expectation. Strong creators generate expectations. Their audience expects attitude, orientation, consistency. These expectations bind not only the creator, but also the system. A strong creator who changes can take large parts of their audience with them. These movements are difficult to predict. Platforms respond to this uncertainty with caution. YouTube prefers channels whose impact is explained by the format, not the person. Formats are stable. They can be replicated.

They don't generate surprises. Personalities, on the other hand, are dynamic. They grow, mature, doubt. These human processes are valuable, but they don't fit well into a system that prioritizes predictability. That's why strong creators are often put in a paradoxical situation. They are successful enough to be relevant, but not so successful that they become dominant. They are seen, but not to the maximum extent. This intermediate position is no coincidence. It is the result of a conscious balance. Many creators respond to this balance by adapting. They tone down their personality, smooth out their statements, and avoid taking clear positions. In the short term, this can increase their reach. In the long term, however, the creator loses their strength. They become predictable again. Predictability is rewarded, but it is not sustainable. It creates interchangeability. Other creators respond with escalation.

They become more provocative, more emotional, more polarizing. They try to break through the limitations. This strategy can generate short-term attention, but almost always leads to even stronger regulation. Escalation confirms the risk that the system wants to avoid. The productive way to deal with this paradox lies neither in adaptation nor in escalation, but in conscious design. Strong creators must learn to modulate their impact. Not to reduce it, but to structure it. Influence can have an effect, but it must remain integrable. This modulation is challenging. It requires self-reflection. It requires an understanding of how one's own presence affects others. Not only individuals, but the system as a whole. Those who ignore this effect will be slowed down. Those who exaggerate it will be slowed down as well. The narrow path between the two is where sustainable growth lies. Understanding why strong creators are paradoxically slowed down takes away the threat of the phenomenon. It explains why success is not linear. Why strength does not automatically lead to greater visibility. And why many of the most influential voices are never the loudest. This section leads to an important insight. Growth is no longer a sign of strength today. It is a sign of compatibility. Strength is not measured by reach, but by depth of impact. Those who accept this can stop measuring themselves by numbers. They can begin to redefine their role. The next section is about how platforms try to transform strong personalities into controllable roles. And why many creators unconsciously go along with this transition without realizing what they are losing in the process.

How personalities are transformed into roles

When platforms cannot stop strength, they try to shape it. This shaping does not happen through prohibitions or clear interventions, but through subtle shifts. Visibility is increased where personalities can be translated into roles. Roles are manageable. They have clear expectations, defined boundaries, and predictable effects. Personalities, on the other hand, are open. They evolve. They cross boundaries. That is precisely why the system tries to transform personality into role. A role is not a mask. It is a functional framework. It reduces complexity. It makes behavior predictable. A creator is no longer seen as a human being, but as an authority. As an explainer. As an entertainer. As a commentator. As an expert. These attributions are not wrong, but they are limiting. They bundle impact in a form that is easier to control. YouTube does not explicitly promote this role formation, but indirectly. Content that clearly corresponds to a role is easier to classify. It fits into existing recommendation clusters. It creates stable usage patterns.

Personal breaks, developmental steps, or changes in perspective disrupt this classification. They increase variance. That is why they are treated more cautiously. Many creators make this transition unconsciously. They notice that certain content works better. That certain statements get more reach. That a certain tone is preferred. They repeat what works. Repetition creates consistency. Consistency solidifies the role. Over time, a spontaneous form of expression becomes an expectation. Expectation becomes obligation. This obligation is subtle. It is not spoken aloud, but it is palpable. The audience reacts with irritation when the creator steps out of character. The system responds with reduced visibility. Both types of feedback reinforce each other. The creator learns to stay within the role. Not because they want to, but because it is easier. Roles have advantages. They provide orientation. They facilitate production. They reduce the pressure to make decisions. But they also come at a price. They limit development. They freeze personality. The creator becomes functional. He fulfills a task. This functionality is systemically attractive, but humanly limiting. Platforms prefer roles because they enable interchangeability. If one creator drops out, another with a similar role can step in. The system remains stable. Personalities, on the other hand, are not replaceable. Their absence creates gaps. Gaps are risky. That is why personality is molded into a form. This molding does not happen by force. It happens through reward. Visibility, monetization, collaborations. Everything that remains within the role is made easier.

Everything that goes beyond it is made more difficult. Many creators interpret this dynamic as a natural maturing process. In truth, it is a process of adaptation. The loss happens gradually. First, doubts disappear. Then ambivalence. Then contradictions. Content becomes clearer, but also smoother. Personality is not erased, but simplified. This simplification increases reach, but it reduces depth. The creator becomes visible, but less alive. For many, this trade-off is acceptable. Visibility for complexity. Security for development. But for creators who work from an inner drive, this trade-off eventually becomes noticeably painful. They notice that they are repeating themselves. That they are meeting expectations instead of asking questions. That their content works, but no longer carries weight. YouTube does not actively enforce this role formation. It merely creates the conditions under which it becomes attractive.

Those who fall out of the role risk visibility. Those who remain in it are rewarded. This logic is not moral. It is functional. Platforms need stability. Roles provide stability. The reason this transition is so effective lies in the psychology of recognition. People react strongly to validation. Reach acts like approval. It signals that you are right. This feedback is powerful. It can guide development without ever being spoken. Creators follow the path of visibility and often realize too late that they have limited themselves in the process. This dynamic explains why many large channels eventually stagnate. The role has been exhausted. Development is no longer possible within the role. The creator is faced with a decision. Either they remain functional and stable, or they risk visibility in order to develop further. This decision is existential because it affects not only reach but also identity. Platforms have no interest in making this decision visible. They benefit from the stability of roles.

But creators who want to have a long-term impact need to be aware of this dynamic. They need to recognize when a role is supportive and when it is limiting. This realization is painful, but necessary. Understanding how personalities are transformed into roles is key to the rest of this book. It shows that reach not only distributes, but also shapes. It changes not only visibility, but also self-image. Those who ignore this quietly lose themselves. Those who recognize it can make conscious choices. The next section reveals why many creators miss the moment when a role begins to control them. And why this moment is decisive for long-term impact.

The moment when the role begins to control you

The transition from personality to role does not happen abruptly. There is no clear cut, no clear signal. That is precisely why it is so dangerous. For a long time, it feels like success. Reach stabilizes. Feedback becomes more positive. Expectations become clearer. The creator feels like they have arrived. But it is precisely at this moment that the relationship begins to reverse. The role that once supported them begins to lead. And at some point, it begins to control them. Control is not manifested in coercion, but in restriction. Topics that used to be taken for granted suddenly feel risky. Thoughts that arise internally are rejected because they do not fit the established line. Language becomes more cautious. Tone becomes smoother. Content no longer arises from inner necessity, but from anticipated expectations. This change is subtle. It is rarely consciously perceived. But it fundamentally changes the inner relationship to one's own work. The decisive moment is not the loss of reach, but the loss of freedom. Many creators do not notice that they have restricted themselves because the external signals remain positive. The numbers are right. The community is responding. Collaborations are emerging. Everything seems to be working.

But internally, a quiet resistance arises. A tiredness. A feeling of repetition. This feeling is often ignored because it seems irrational. After all, things are going well. YouTube indirectly reinforces this state of affairs. Content that stays within the role is preferred. Content that challenges it is treated more cautiously. This feedback is not clear enough to be recognized as a restriction, but it is consistent enough to shape behavior. The creator learns what works and what doesn't. Not through rules, but through experience. The moment the role begins to control is often the moment when development would be necessary. People evolve. Perspectives shift. Questions change. But the role remains the same. It is frozen. This discrepancy creates tension. Tension that cannot be openly expressed finds other outlets. It manifests itself as cynicism, distance, overproduction, or withdrawal. Many creators respond to this tension with rationalization. They tell themselves that they must be professional. That they owe it to their audience to remain consistent. That personal development should not be a priority.

These thoughts are understandable. They are also partly correct. But they obscure the real conflict. The conflict is not between professionalism and authenticity, but between growth and control. The role controls not only content, but also perception. The creator begins to see themselves through the role. They evaluate their thoughts according to whether they fit. They filter their language. They adjust their attitude. This self-regulation is efficient, but it is also draining. It reduces inner diversity. However, diversity is the source of development. YouTube has no interest in making this control transparent. It is a by-product of a logic that favors stability. Roles are stable. Personalities are dynamic. Dynamism creates uncertainty. Uncertainty is avoided. This chain is not personal, but structural. Yet for the creator, it feels personal because it affects their own freedom of expression. The most dangerous aspect of this control is its invisibility. There is no moment when you can say, now it's too much. It is a creeping process. Each individual step is small, understandable, reasonable. Only in retrospect does it become clear how far one has strayed. Not from the platform, but from oneself. Many creators miss this moment because they do not recognize it as a problem. They confuse stability with consistency. They confuse reach with resonance. But resonance feels different.

It is alive. It surprises. It challenges. Stability, on the other hand, is calm, predictable, safe. Security is comfortable, but it is no substitute for development. The moment when the role begins to take control is therefore a turning point. It determines whether a creator remains functional or continues to develop. This decision is not easy because it involves risks. Development can cost reach. It can cause irritation. It can trigger uncertainty. But stagnation costs more in the long run. It costs substance. YouTube does not actively punish development. It merely reacts cautiously. This caution is often perceived as rejection. But it is a signal. A signal that something new is emerging that has not yet been classified. Those who misinterpret this signal return to their role. Those who interpret it correctly endure the moment. Enduring means working with uncertainty. Not optimizing immediately. Not smoothing things out immediately. Instead, giving the new space to breathe. This attitude is difficult in a system that is accustomed to quick feedback. But it is necessary if personality is not to become frozen in function.

The moment of control is also the moment of choice. Do you remain predictable or do you come alive again? Both paths are legitimate. But they lead to different forms of impact. Predictability brings visibility. Liveliness brings depth. The question is not which is better, but what you want. Chapter five thus approaches its inner core. It is not about guilt, not about resistance, not about fighting against the platform. It is about awareness. Awareness of the forces at work. Awareness of the decisions you make, often without realizing it. This thought will be concluded in the next section. It is about how creators can preserve their personality without falling out of the system. Not through rebellion, but through conscious positioning. Where impact remains possible without losing control.

How to preserve personality without falling out of the system

Preserving personality does not mean resisting the system. Resistance creates friction, friction creates attention, attention creates escalation. Escalation is regulated. Those who work against the system reinforce the very mechanisms they want to avoid. Personality is not preserved through struggle, but through positioning. Through a conscious way of standing in the system without being shaped by it. The crucial difference lies in the inner reference. Roles are oriented outward. They respond to expectations, to numbers, to feedback. Personality is oriented inward. It arises from an attitude, not from a function. Those who keep this inner reference clear can adapt to the outside world without losing themselves internally. This separation is subtle, but it is possible. YouTube does not demand impersonality. It demands legibility. Legibility does not mean simplifying oneself, but structuring oneself. Personality becomes problematic when it is unrestrained. When it is erratic, contradictory without context, emotional without context. Personality that is guided can be integrated. Personality that is left to its own devices seems risky. Guidance does not mean control in a negative sense. It means awareness. Awareness of the effect you create. The states you open up. The expectations you set. This awareness allows you to show personality without overwhelming the system. It allows development without creating chaos. Many creators believe they have to choose. Either authentic or successful. Either themselves or visible. This dichotomy is false. It arises from a misunderstanding of authenticity. Authenticity is not the equation of the inner and the outer. It is the alignment of attitude and expression.

Expression can be shaped without betraying one's attitude. YouTube does not respond to truth or untruth. It responds to impact. Those who show their personality in a way that allows its impact to remain legible can grow. Legible does not mean harmless. It means structured. A thought can be deep if it is supported. An emotion can be strong if it is framed. Development can be visible if it is comprehensible. The key lies in the timing. Personality does not unfold in isolated moments, but as a process. Those who stage development as a series of leaps create irritation. Those who show development as a path create orientation. Orientation calms. Calm enables visibility. This chain is not intuitive, but it is effective. Many creators lose their personality not because they adapt, but because they fail to translate their inner dynamics. They speak from inner emotion without giving the audience a foothold. This rawness is human, but systemically demanding. Translation does not mean falsification. It means mediation. Those who mediate lose nothing.

They make themselves accessible. Personality is preserved when it is not linked to reaction. As soon as personality depends on feedback, it becomes a role. The creator begins to observe themselves. They measure their authenticity by their reach. This mechanism is fatal because it shifts the inner reference point. Personality then becomes performative. It is made, not lived. The way out lies in a clear inner separation. Content serves communication. Personality serves as orientation. Those who do not mix these levels remain free. They can adapt content without compromising themselves. They can change formats without losing themselves. They can grow or stagnate without making their identity dependent on it. YouTube tolerates personality as long as it does not become dominant. Dominance arises when personality has an unfiltered effect on the space. Integration arises when personality has a structured effect. This structure is not a restriction, but a protection. It protects the system from overload and the creator from losing themselves. Many of the most enduring creators have intuitively understood this point. They are not loud. They are clear. They evolve, but they mark their evolution. They change their perspective, but they take their audience with them. They allow ambivalence, but they frame it. This attitude is not spectacular, but it is sustainable. How personality is preserved without falling out of the system is not a technique. It is an inner attitude. An attitude of self-responsibility.

Not in the sense of self-optimization, but in the sense of self-leadership. Those who can lead themselves do not have to be led by the system. Chapter five ends here because a central tension has become apparent at this point. YouTube does not limit personality, but uncontrollability. Strong creators are not slowed down because they are wrong, but because they are effective. Roles do not arise because platforms manipulate, but because stability is required. Those who understand these connections can make conscious decisions. They can preserve their personality without isolating themselves. They can grow without losing themselves. This ability is rare, but it can be learned. And it is the key to a sustainable presence on a platform that no longer amplifies but regulates. In chapter six, we will explore this idea further. It shows why artificial intelligence today is less a recommendation system than a control instrument. And why this understanding will determine whether creators grow or remain invisible in the future.

Notes:

Notes:

Chapter 6: AI as an instrument of stabilization

Why AI now exercises control and no longer just makes recommendations

Artificial intelligence has long been portrayed as a neutral helper. As a tool that recognizes patterns, understands interests, and brings content to where it fits. This idea was helpful as long as recommendation was synonymous with distribution. But with the growth of platforms, the function of AI has shifted. It no longer primarily makes recommendations. It regulates. And regulation is a form of control. Not repressive, not visible, but structural. YouTube now uses AI not to distribute content as widely as possible, but to contain its effects. The task of AI is no longer to find the best, but the most compatible. Compatibility is not a content-related criterion. It is a systemic one. It describes how well content can be integrated into existing usage patterns without destabilizing them.

AI is the ideal tool for this because it does not think, it compares. AI does not evaluate ideas. It evaluates deviations. It does not recognize what is new, but what deviates from the expected. Deviation is not a mistake, but it is a risk. The greater the deviation, the more intense the observation. The more intense the observation, the more cautious the scaling. This logic is emotionless, but consistent. It explains why innovative content is often slowed down while familiar formats grow. AI does not work at the level of individual videos. It works at the level of patterns. It reads histories, chains, repetitions. It recognizes how user states change. It compares these changes with millions of other histories. The goal is not optimization, but stabilization. AI becomes a tool that dampens deviations before they become systemically relevant. Many creators underestimate this function because they still understand AI as a recommendation system. They believe you have to please AI. But AI has no preferences. It has thresholds. It does not work with taste, but with tolerances. Within these tolerances, many things are possible. Outside of them, there are limitations. These limitations are not personal. They are statistical. AI does not control content, but dynamics. It does not ask what is being said, but what is happening. How is behavior changing? How are usage paths changing? How are emotional states changing? These changes are evaluated. Content that triggers too strong shifts is contained.

Not banned, not deleted, but slowed down. Slowness is a form of control. It reduces reach without triggering resistance. It does not seem like censorship, but rather like market logic. A video remains visible, but it does not explode. A channel grows, but not exponentially. This form of limitation is efficient because it is invisible. It does not cause scandals. It only causes frustration. AI is not the actor here, but rather the tool. The goals are predetermined: stability, security, predictability. AI implements these goals because it recognizes patterns faster than humans. It sees where something could tip over long before it tips over. This early warning function is central to platforms that can no longer afford surprises. For creators, this reality is difficult to accept because it challenges the idea of fairness. One wants to believe that good content will find its way. But AI does not evaluate quality. It evaluates fit.

Fit with a system that has to sustain itself. This fit can be shaped, but it's not arbitrary. Those who understand AI as a control tool stop fighting it. They also stop idealizing it. They start to read it. They no longer ask how they can please AI, but how their content works. Impact is what AI recognizes. Not intention. Not quality. Not effort. This realization shifts the focus. Away from optimization and toward awareness. Those who work consciously can design within the tolerances. They can sense boundaries without testing them. They can have an impact without causing escalation. This ability is not technical. It is psychological. Chapter six therefore does not begin with technology, but with a change of roles. AI is no longer a partner. It is a regulator. It ensures that the system works. Those who understand this can stop hoping for old promises. They can begin to work in a new reality. The next section reveals why AI does not evaluate content, but states. And why this state evaluation is the key to understanding reach from 2026 onwards.

Why AI evaluates states rather than content

Artificial intelligence does not work with meaning. It works with correlation. It does not recognize truths, but patterns of behavior. This is precisely why its use on YouTube has shifted so fundamentally. AI no longer asks what content says, but what it triggers in people. Not in words, but in states. These states have become the actual control object of the platform. A state is not a feeling in the classic sense. It is a combination of attention, arousal, orientation, and willingness to act. AI recognizes this combination indirectly, through behavior. Through click intervals, dwell time patterns, pauses, switching speed, and recurrence. These signals create a picture. This picture is not individual, but statistical. It shows the state users are in after consumption. YouTube is now less interested in content than in these state images. Content is only a trigger. The real value lies in the effect afterwards. A video can be harmless in terms of content and still create a state that is considered unstable. Another can be complex and still be calming. AI does not distinguish by topic, but by consequence. This state assessment is the reason why classic content analyses come to nothing.

Creators analyze titles, thumbnails, lengths, and topics. AI analyzes transitions. It asks what happens between two videos. Whether a user continues smoothly or stops abruptly. Whether they remain calm or become hectic. These transitions are more decisive than anything that happens in the video itself. A stable state is valuable for the platform. It shows that the user remains integrated. That they are not overwhelmed. That they do not switch off. AI recognizes stability as consistency. Consistency in behavior. Consistency in usage. Content that promotes such consistency is read as compatible. It is allowed to grow. Unstable states, on the other hand, are risky. They manifest themselves in sharp fluctuations. Very long watch time followed by abandonment. Many clicks with a short dwell time. Intense comments followed by a stop in usage.

These patterns signal overload or friction. AI does not respond to this with prohibition, but with limitation. This logic explains why some content is not scaled despite high interaction. It creates states that cannot be integrated. It leaves people emotionally open, agitated, searching. This can be valuable for the individual. For the system, it is problematic. AI does not read value, but risk. States are therefore the real lever of the platform. YouTube tries to keep users in an optimal state. Not euphoric, not bored, not irritated. A state of medium activation, high orientation, and low friction is considered ideal. AI optimizes for this state, not for content. This optimization is not evil. It is functional. A platform with billions of users must regulate states in order to remain stable. AI is the only tool that can react quickly enough to do this. It recognizes patterns before they become visible. It dampens before things escalate. For creators, this means a radical shift.

Success no longer comes from what you say, but from what you leave behind. The state after the video is more decisive than the moment of consumption. Those who stir people up without guiding them create instability. Those who guide people without captivating them create stability. Many creators underestimate this aftereffect. They focus on the climax of the video. On the powerful moment. On the punchline. But AI is interested in what comes after. In the transition. For the integration. A video that ends strongly but offers no internal conclusion leaves open states. Open states are difficult to integrate. State evaluation also explains why calm content often grows. Not because it is boring, but because it closes states. It guides people through a thought and leaves them feeling organized. This order is systemically valuable. It allows for continued consumption. It reduces dropouts. It stabilizes usage. AI reads these effects over time. Not immediately. Not in the first test. It observes how states repeat themselves. Whether a channel reliably generates similar states. This reliability is crucial. A channel that consistently generates calming, orienting states is read as safe. Security is a prerequisite for scaling. Instability, on the other hand, is not punished, but limited. Content remains visible, but it is not widely distributed. It is allowed to exist, but it must not dominate. This logic is difficult to accept because it is invisible. But it is consistent. Understanding why AI evaluates states rather than content is key to the rest of this book. It explains why so many well-intentioned strategies come to nothing. They optimize content, while AI reads states. They improve interfaces, while the system regulates effects. The next section reveals why this state logic leads to certain forms of depth becoming systemically problematic. And why exactly this depth remains possible when it is designed differently.

Why depth becomes a risk when it offers no support

Depth is not an objective value. It is an experience. It arises where content not only informs, but also moves us internally. Where it triggers thought processes, shifts perspectives, and challenges self-images. This kind of depth is valuable to humans. It is the core of education, reflection, and personal development. But it is precisely this depth that becomes a risk in the context of a stability-oriented system when it offers no support. Support means orientation. An inner railing that the viewer can hold on to while something is moving. Depth without support opens up spaces, but leaves them unstructured. People are left with questions without knowing how to hold on to them. For the individual, this can be a productive state. For a system that manages billions of users at the same time, it is problematic. Unsupported depth creates states that are difficult to integrate. AI does not recognize these states as depth, but as instability. It sees that users pause, abort, become restless, or fall out of the usage path after such content. These reactions are not an evaluation of the content, but a signal about its after-effects.

Depth that offers no support creates open loops. Open loops are systemically expensive. That is why depth is not limited per se, but contextualized. Content with high depth is scaled when it also offers structure. Structure does not mean simplification. It means guidance. A thought can be complex if it is developed in a comprehensible way. A question can remain open if it is clear in which space it stands. Depth becomes acceptable when it does not cause disorientation. Many creators confuse depth with openness. They believe that true depth must not provide answers. That it must be irritating. That it should be disturbing. This attitude is philosophically understandable. But it is systemically demanding. Content that deliberately destabilizes creates conditions that the system cannot support. It is not deleted, but it is limited. Stability comes from inner order. From clear lines, even if they are not definitive. From language that guides rather than distracts. From a rhythm that builds tension and then releases it. These elements make depth integrable. They allow the viewer to move without losing themselves. AI prefers depth that closes.

Not in the sense of final answers, but in the sense of psychological rounding off. A video may open up questions if it embeds them at the end. It may sow doubts if it offers a framework in which these doubts can be held. This ability is rare, but it is crucial. Depth without support acts like an abyss. Depth with support acts like a path. The difference lies not in the content, but in the design. The abyss attracts, but it lets you fall. The path challenges, but it carries you. Systems prefer paths. They avoid abysses. Not out of fear, but out of responsibility. For creators, this presents a new challenge. They must learn to guide depth. Not to dose it, but to structure it. This structure is not a betrayal of complexity. It is its prerequisite. Without structure, depth is not read, but limited. Many creators only experience this connection in retrospect. They see that their deepest content has the least reach. They interpret this as a rejection of depth. But in truth, it is a rejection of instability. Depth that carries can grow. Depth that overwhelms becomes isolated. This insight is central to understanding reach from 2026 onwards. It shows that it is not the intensity of a thought that matters, but its ability to be integrated. Integration is the new keyword. Content does not have to be shallow. It has to be integrable. The next section reveals why AI is particularly sensitive to ambiguity. And why unframed ambiguity has become one of the biggest obstacles to growth for sophisticated content.

Why unframed ambiguity blocks growth

Ambiguity is a strength of human thinking. It allows for ambiguity, openness, and changes in perspective. It tolerates contradictions without immediately resolving them. Ambiguity is a central element in art, philosophy, and personal development. But in an algorithmically regulated system, it becomes a problem if it remains unframed. Not because it is wrong, but because it is difficult to integrate. Unframed ambiguity creates uncertainty. It leaves the viewer without orientation. Not in an intellectual sense, but in a psychological sense. People sense that something is open, but they don't know how open. They don't know whether to think further, switch off, or hold on. This ambiguity creates conditions that are not stable. AI reads these states as friction. Friction is not a mistake.

It is a signal. It shows that content does not fit smoothly into existing usage patterns. In an open system, this would be a sign of innovation. In a stability-oriented system, it is a risk. AI responds to this by limiting its reach. Not to prohibit ambiguity, but to control its spread. The problem lies not in ambiguity itself, but in its lack of context. Ambiguity without context is like an open space without walls. People don't know where they stand. Ambiguity with context, on the other hand, is like a space with clear contours in which one can move freely. The difference is crucial. Context provides support without destroying openness. Many creators underestimate this effect. They believe that ambiguity per se signals depth. They leave questions unanswered without contextualizing them. They play with contradictions without resolving them. This content is intellectually challenging, but psychologically demanding. AI does not recognize this demand as a value, but as a burden.

Unframed ambiguity often leads to pauses. Viewers stop consuming to think. These pauses are valuable to humans. They show that something has had an impact. But they are problematic for the system because they interrupt the usage path. AI measures these interruptions and responds with restraint. This does not mean that ambiguity must disappear. It must be guided. Guidance means consciously marking ambiguity. Signaling to the viewer that openness is intentional. That there is no immediate conclusion, but a framework in which openness exists. These signals can be set linguistically, structurally, or rhythmically. One example is the clear naming of areas of tension. Not to resolve them, but to make them visible. Visibility reduces uncertainty. Another example is embedding ambiguity in a narrative movement. The viewer is guided, even if the destination remains open. This guidance creates trust. AI responds positively to such forms of ambiguity because they create states that are open but stable. Stability does not mean unambiguity.

It means sustainability. A state is sustainable if it does not escalate, does not overwhelm, and does not disorient. Ambiguity can be sustainable when it is framed. Many of the most successful in-depth content on YouTube works exactly like this. They ask questions without providing definitive answers. They leave room for interpretation, but they provide support through structure. This content does not grow explosively, but it grows steadily. It generates resonance without instability. Unframed ambiguity, on the other hand, remains isolated. It reaches a small, highly engaged audience, but does not scale. This isolation is often interpreted as a sign of exclusivity. In reality, it is a protective mechanism of the system.

It prevents open states from being generated en masse. Understanding why unframed ambiguity blocks growth is particularly important for creators who work at a high level. It shows that depth does not have to be reduced, but rather guided. It shows that openness does not have to disappear, but can be structured. This structure is not a compromise, but an act of translation. The next section will clarify why this act of translation determines whether AI classifies content as compatible or risky. And why creators who master this translation have a decisive advantage without losing their substance.

How depth can be translated without losing its power

Translation is not betrayal. It is a form of responsibility. Anyone who experiences something profound intuitively senses that this depth cannot be carried raw into every context without causing damage. This is precisely where the new challenge for creators comes in. Depth can remain. It just has to become translatable. Translatable not in the sense of simplification, but in the sense of connectivity. Translatability means that impact takes on a form. A form that can be maintained. Depth does not lose its power when it is guided. It only loses its power when it is fragmented or diluted.

Guidance is different from smoothing. Guidance provides direction without specifying a destination. It creates a space in which depth can have an effect without being overwhelming. AI responds positively to translated depth because it creates states that are both open and stable. Stability here does not mean stagnation, but rather sustainability. A viewer may be moved internally as long as this movement is embedded. Translation is precisely this embedding. It makes visible what otherwise remains implicit. Many creators believe that depth must be self-explanatory. That it is only real when it occurs abruptly. This idea is romantic, but it misjudges the level of impact. Abrupt depth catches people off guard. It opens up spaces without transition. For some, this is liberating. For many, it is overwhelming. AI does not recognize this overwhelm as depth, but as instability. Translation therefore begins before depth.

It begins with context. The viewer needs to know what space they are entering. Not in terms of content, but emotionally. Will it be calm or demanding? Will it be open or focused? These signals prepare the viewer. Preparation reduces friction. Friction is what blocks growth. Another aspect of translation is rhythm. Depth needs pauses. Not pauses in the sense of interruption, but in the sense of integration. One thought must be allowed to take effect before the next one comes. These pauses are guided, not empty.

They provide space without losing orientation. AI recognizes this rhythm as stabilizing. Language is also a translation tool. Not by simplifying, but by structuring. Complex thoughts can be formulated clearly. Clarity reduces uncertainty. Uncertainty is the enemy of scaling. Clarity is its ally. Depth that is clearly expressed is no less profound. It is more accessible. Many creators fear that translation will make their content banal. But the opposite is true. Untranslated depth reaches few and remains isolated. Translated depth reaches more people and has a more lasting effect. It changes not only individuals, but groups. This change is quieter, but it is broader. AI prefers precisely this form of impact. Not explosive insights, but integrable ones. Not shocks, but processes. Depth becomes systemically acceptable when it appears as a path, not an abyss. The path challenges, but it carries. The abyss pulls, but it lets fall. Systems choose paths. For creators, this means a new mastery.

Not just thinking about content, but shaping impact. Not just experiencing depth, but communicating it. This communication is not a technical trick. It is an attitude. An attitude of responsibility towards the audience and towards one's own impact. Those who make depth translatable lose none of its power. They gain reach without chasing it. They remain intact without isolating themselves. They do not work against AI, but within its logic, without submitting to it. This ability is rare, but it can be learned. Chapter six ends here because at this point a central misunderstanding has been resolved. AI does not limit depth. It limits groundlessness. It does not limit personality. It limits uncontrollability. Those who understand this can begin to shape depth in such a way that it has an effect and grows. It shows why content with meaning can become systemically dangerous. And why precisely this danger is the key to a new, quiet growth model that will work from 2026 onwards.

Notes:

Notes:

Chapter 7: Why depth has become risky

Why meaning is more dangerous than superficiality

Meaning is not a harmless state. It has lasting effects. It changes not only what people know, but how they see themselves, others, and the world. That is precisely why meaning is systemically more delicate than superficiality. Superficial content touches without changing. Meaningful content changes without immediately closing again. For a system that prioritizes stability, this aftereffect is risky. YouTube has no problem with entertainment. Entertainment is fleeting. It leaves hardly any traces. It activates briefly and then dissolves again. Meaning, on the other hand, leaves traces. It continues to work even when the screen has long been turned off. People think, doubt, rearrange. These processes are valuable individually, but difficult to control collectively. Meaning generates movement beyond the platform. And that is precisely what makes it dangerous. Dangerous not in a moral sense, but in a systemic sense. Meaning eludes control because it is not bound to the medium. It has an effect in everyday life, in conversations, in decisions.

Platforms cannot measure what happens outside their boundaries. They can only observe that usage is interrupted, that pauses occur, that people do not return immediately. These effects are interpreted as instability. Superficiality is predictable. It generates short stimuli, quick reactions, clear patterns. Meaning is unpredictable. It can be reassuring or unsettling. It can connect or divide. It can strengthen or unsettle. This ambivalence is the core of its power. And it is precisely this ambivalence that makes systems cautious. Many creators believe that meaning is automatically rewarded. That content that says something must grow. This assumption stems from a time when platforms were designed for discovery. Today, they are designed for management. Management prefers states that can be closed. Meaning cannot be closed. It remains open. YouTube responds to meaning not with rejection, but with limitation. Content with high meaning is not deleted, but slowed down. It is distributed in smaller circles. It is allowed to have an effect, but it should not have a mass effect. This dosage is not a judgment on its value. It is a protective mechanism.

Meaning becomes particularly problematic when it is ambiguous. When it asks questions instead of providing answers. When it triggers internal processes without guiding them. These forms of meaning create states that are difficult to integrate. AI recognizes these states and responds with caution. Reach remains limited, even though resonance is high. The paradox is that it is precisely this content that is the real reason many creators make content. They want to say something. They want to move people. They want to create meaning. And it is precisely this motivation that brings them into conflict with a platform that regulates impact. This conflict cannot be resolved, but it can be shaped. Meaning becomes more systemically acceptable when it is embedded. When it appears not as a break, but as a process. When it does not shock, but accompanies. This embedding does not change the meaning itself, but its form. Form determines scalability. Many creators underestimate the power of form. They focus on what they want to say, not how it comes across. But meaning arises not only from content, but also from context. Context is what the system reads.

A meaningful thought in a stable context can be integrated. The same thought without context is limited. Understanding why meaning is more dangerous than superficiality is not a call for conformity. It is a call for awareness. Those who want to create meaning are responsible for its impact. Not in a moral sense, but in a systemic sense. This responsibility determines whether meaning remains isolated or is allowed to grow. Chapter seven therefore begins not with strategies, but with a reality check. Meaning is powerful. Power is regulated. Those who accept this can stop wondering about limitations. They can begin to shape meaning in such a way that it has an effect without overburdening the system. The next section reveals why content with meaning is often read as too independent. And why it is precisely this independence that is the point where reach ends and impact begins.

Why independence is the point where reach ends

Independence is the moment when content stops leaning on something else. It no longer copies, it no longer reacts, it no longer just explains. It stands on its own. This is exactly where meaning begins. And this is exactly where reach often ends. Not because independence is wrong, but because it eludes the logic of the system. Independent content does not need a reference. It does not explain itself through trends, formats, or existing discourses. It arises from an inner necessity. This necessity is palpable to people. It creates depth, trust, and resonance. But for a system based on comparison and classification, independence is difficult to read. It does not fit into existing categories. It does not create clear clusters. It is singular. YouTube works with similarity. Recommendations arise where content is comparable. Where topics, tonalities, and effects overlap. Independent content interrupts this logic. It resembles nothing else. It cannot simply be placed next to something else. This incomparability is its strength, but also its systemic problem.

Content that clearly follows an existing pattern can be easily distributed. The system knows who it can show it to. Unique content forces the system to test. Testing creates uncertainty. Uncertainty is limited. That's why reach often ends where content becomes too unique. Many creators experience this point as an invisible wall. They notice that their content is becoming more mature. Clearer. More personal. Less conformist. And at the same time, they notice that growth is not happening. This simultaneity is no coincidence. It is an expression of a transition. The transition from dissemination to impact. Independence creates impact because it does not confirm, but challenges. It offers no familiar patterns, but new perspectives. People who engage with it do so consciously. This conscious decision reduces mass. Reach thrives on automatism. Impact thrives on decision. These two principles contradict each other. YouTube favors automatism. Autoplay, recommendations, next videos. Everything is designed to minimize decisions. Independent content requires decisions. Should I engage with it?

Should I stay? Should I think about it? These decisions interrupt the flow. Interruption is systemically expensive. That is why independence is not scaled, but isolated. It finds its audience, but it is not distributed en masse. This audience is often highly engaged, loyal, and resonant. But it remains limited. This limitation is not a judgment on quality, but a consequence of the system's logic. Many creators try to circumvent this limitation by disguising originality. They package new ideas in old formats. They use familiar structures to introduce unfamiliar content. This strategy can work as long as originality does not dominate. But it has its limits. At some point, the break becomes visible. The point at which reach ends is therefore not a failure. It is a marker. It shows that content is no longer being consumed, but processed. Processing takes time. Time is what the system cannot provide indefinitely. Reach is fast. Impact is slow. Originality slows things down. It draws attention away from the flow. It demands presence. This presence is precious, but it is not scalable in the traditional sense. YouTube does not recognize this preciousness as an advantage, but as a risk. Risk is regulated. This does not mean that independent content must remain invisible. It means that it grows differently. Not through explosion, but through condensation. Not through mass, but through depth.

This growth is less spectacular, but it is more sustainable. Understanding why independence is the point where reach ends changes the view of success. Success is no longer about reaching as many people as possible, but about reaching the right people. People who are willing to engage. These people don't come by chance. They come through resonance. Resonance is not an algorithmic goal. It is a human one. But systems cannot maximize resonance without becoming unstable. That is why it is limited. Not out of rejection, but out of necessity. Chapter seven thus reveals another boundary. A boundary that many creators reach without being able to name it. The boundary between visibility and significance. Those who recognize this boundary can stop trying to break through it. They can begin to work along its line. The next section reveals why this line is precisely the place where a new growth model is emerging. A model that is quieter, slower, but more sustainable. And why creators who understand this will have an advantage in 2026.

Why impact is slower than reach

Reach is an event. Impact is a process. This difference is crucial to understanding why growth feels different today than it did in the past. Reach happens quickly. It is visible, measurable, comparable. Impact, on the other hand, unfolds slowly. It works in the background. It doesn't immediately change behavior, but rather perception. It is precisely this slowness that makes impact valuable and systemically difficult. Platforms are optimized for events. A video goes viral. Numbers rise. Attention is focused. These dynamics can be measured, controlled, and monetized. Impact eludes this access. It does not manifest itself in the moment, but rather in the aftermath. People think further. They change perspectives. They make different decisions. These changes are real, but they are not immediately visible. They are difficult to manage for a system that relies on real-time control. YouTube prefers reach because it responds quickly. Impact, on the other hand, takes time. Time means uncertainty. Uncertainty means risk. That is why impact is not actively promoted. It is tolerated as long as it remains limited.

This tolerance is not a lack of appreciation. It is a consequence of the system architecture. Many creators confuse this slowness with failure. They see no explosion, no peaks, no quick wins. They believe their content is not working. In reality, it is working on a different level. It is having an impact, but it is not growing. This divergence between impact and growth is one of the key features of YouTube from 2026 onwards. Impact changes people, but it does not change them synchronously. Each viewer processes content at their own pace. Some need days, others weeks, others months. This asynchronous processing is human. However, it is difficult for the system to integrate. Algorithms work synchronously. They compare patterns in short time windows. Slow processes fall outside this grid. That's why content that has a slow impact often isn't scaled. It doesn't fit into the platform's logic of acceleration.

It doesn't generate clear signals. It's quiet. Quiet signals get lost in the noise. Not because they're weak, but because they work differently. Impact is also not cumulative in the same sense as reach. Reach adds up. Impact intensifies. Ten people who are deeply moved are not the same as a thousand people who take a quick look. This condensation is qualitative, not quantitative. Systems favor quantity because it is comparable. Quality is difficult to compare. It eludes simple rankings. YouTube often recognizes impact only indirectly. Through long-term loyalty. Through return visits.

Through stable communities. These effects are valuable, but they are not spectacular. They do not generate viral stories. They are difficult to market. That is why they are not treated as a primary growth target. Many creators face a decision at this point. They can try to accelerate impact by sharpening, emotionalizing, or simplifying content. Or they can accept that impact takes time. This acceptance is difficult because it requires patience. Patience is not a popular value in an attention economy. Slowing down impact means detaching yourself from comparison. It means not interpreting every fluctuation. It means developing trust in the process. This trust is not naive. It is based on the realization that not everything that matters is visible. And that visibility is not everything that matters. YouTube will never be able to fully promote impact without destabilizing itself. That's why impact will always remain a borderline case. It can exist, but it cannot dominate. This boundary is frustrating, but it is real. Those who ignore it are fighting against the system. Those who accept it can work within it. Slow impact has an advantage that fast reach does not have. It is more resilient. People who are reached through impact stay. They are less dependent on trends. They are less volatile. This stability is valuable to humans, even if it is not maximally rewarded algorithmically.

Understanding why impact is slower than reach helps creators adjust their expectations. It explains why growth is no longer linear. Why pauses occur. Why nothing seems to happen, even though a lot is happening. This insight takes the pressure off. It allows for a different approach to time. The next section reveals why this slowness is the key to a new growth model. A model that relies not on explosions, but on consolidation. And why this model will be the only sustainable option for many creators from 2026 onwards.

Why quiet growth is systemically preferred

Quiet growth does not attract attention. It does not generate headlines, viral curves, or sudden spikes. That is precisely why it is attractive to the system. Quiet growth does not destabilize anything. It does not abruptly shift the balance of power. It does not create excessive demands. It integrates itself. And integration is the central goal of a platform that must sustain itself. YouTube has learned that loud successes are expensive. They attract attention, but they also entail risks. Rapid growth brings pressure to perform. Pressure to perform creates escalation. Escalation increases the likelihood of missteps, controversies, and emotional overload. Each of these consequences is systemically problematic. Quiet growth avoids these chain reactions. Quiet growth occurs where content does not explode, but rather takes root. It is not seen by many people immediately, but rather by the right people over and over again.

This recurrence is crucial. It shows that content is not only consumed, but also integrated. Integration is a sign of compatibility. Compatibility is rewarded. Platforms prefer growth that they don't have to explain. A viral hit requires explanation. Why now? Why this topic? Why this person? Every explanation raises questions. Questions create uncertainty. Uncertainty is a risk. Quiet growth doesn't raise questions. It just happens. It is consistent. Consistency is controllable. YouTube measures this quiet growth not by peaks, but by stability. A channel that grows slowly but steadily is seen as safe. Safety is a prerequisite for openness. Openness does not mean explosion, but more leeway. This leeway manifests itself in slightly expanded recommendations, longer test phases, and more stable playouts. Many creators underestimate this dynamic because it is unspectacular. They feel overlooked, even though they are being carried along. They see others exploding and believe they are doing something wrong. But explosions are not the goal of the system. They are by-products that are accepted but not sought after. Quiet growth fits in with the logic of state regulation. Content that appears calm creates stable states. Stable states can be repeated. Repeatability is economically valuable. It enables forecasts. Forecasts enable planning. Planning is the basis of every large platform. This growth is not slow because it is weak. It is slow because it is integrated. Integration takes time. Content must find its place. It must be embedded in existing usage paths. This embedding takes place step by step. Each stage is observed. Each expansion is reviewed. Quiet growth has another advantage.

It protects creators. Those who grow slowly have time to adapt internally. They are not overwhelmed by expectations. They can clarify their stance, find their voice, and solidify their structure. This inner stability is rare, but it is crucial for long-term impact. YouTube favors creators who can support themselves. Supporting themselves means that they are not dependent on short-term attention. That they don't have to escalate to remain relevant. That they don't break down when numbers fluctuate. This resilience is systemically valuable because it reduces failures. Quiet growth is therefore not a coincidence, but a strategy. Not in the sense of a plan, but in the sense of a selection logic. Those who remain calm remain visible. Those who explode are observed. Those who fluctuate too much are limited. This logic is not fair, but it is consistent. Many creators find quiet growth frustrating because it contradicts the cultural ideal of success. Success should be visible. Measurable.

Comparable. Quiet growth eludes this ideal. It seems inconspicuous. But it is resilient. Resilience is what systems seek. Understanding why quiet growth is systemically preferred changes the perspective on success. Success is no longer about becoming as big as possible as quickly as possible. Success is about becoming sustainable. Sustainable for the system. Sustainable for the audience. Sustainable for oneself. The next section will clarify why this quiet growth is not a compromise, but rather the basis of a new growth model. A model that does not work against the platform, but with it, without submitting to it.

The new growth model of consolidation

Consolidation is the opposite of expansion. Expansion spreads out, consolidation collects. Expansion wants more, consolidation wants deeper. In the logic of YouTube from 2026 onwards, consolidation is the more stable growth model. Not because it thinks smaller, but because it is more sustainable. Consolidation means not spreading impact, but bundling it. Not in terms of mass, but in terms of meaning. This growth model emerges where reach is no longer the primary goal. Where content is not designed to reach as many people as possible, but to have as clear an impact as possible. Clarity generates return. Return generates trust. Trust generates loyalty. This loyalty is not exclusive, but it is stable. And stability is what the system can read and carry. Consolidation is not reflected in peaks, but in continuity. A channel does not grow in leaps and bounds, but steadily. Content does not go viral, but becomes relevant. Relevance is not a loud state. It is reflected in the fact that people stay.

That they come back. That they listen, even when nothing spectacular is happening. This form of attention is rare, but it is resilient. YouTube recognizes consolidation indirectly. Through consistent watch time. Through stable return rates. Through comments that don't react, but reflect. Through usage patterns that don't escalate, but settle. These signals are unspectacular, but they are clear. They show that content is being integrated. The new growth model favors creators who don't get carried away. Who don't react to every fluctuation. Who don't try to force attention. This calmness is no coincidence. It is a form of self-management. Self-managed creators generate less systemic friction. Less friction means more leeway. Consolidation also means that content builds on each other.

Not thematically, but in terms of impact. Each piece of content deepens a state rather than opening up a new one. Viewers don't constantly move in new directions, but sink deeper into a space. This space becomes familiar. Familiarity reduces uncertainty. Uncertainty is what blocks scaling. Many creators confuse consolidation with niche. But consolidation is not a restriction in terms of content. It is impact-related. A condensed channel can be thematically broad as long as the inner attitude remains consistent. This consistency is the real anchor. It makes content readable without standardizing it. The new growth model rewards patience. Not in a moral sense, but in a structural sense. Patience means giving the system time to read the impact. Impact is not immediate. It needs repetition. Repetition requires trust. Trust is not created through optimization, but through consistency. Consolidation is also a protective mechanism for creators. Those who work in a consolidated manner are less dependent on external signals. They measure success not by individual videos, but by the development of the space they create. This space becomes more stable over time.

Stability reduces pressure. Reduced pressure allows for better content. This feedback loop is crucial. YouTube prefers this model because it minimizes risk. Condensed channels do not escalate. They polarize less. They generate fewer extreme states. They are predictable without being boring. This combination is rare, but it is valuable. The new growth model of condensation is not a compromise. It is a response to a changed reality. In a platform that regulates rather than amplifies, growth can no longer be explosive without being limited. Condensation circumvents this limit by not challenging it. Creators who understand this model stop chasing reach. They start building spaces. These spaces grow slowly, but they last. They carry meaning without tipping over. They allow personality without creating dominance. They are integrable. Chapter seven ends here because at this point, a new image of success has become visible. Success is no longer volume, but sustainability. Not speed, but density. Not reach, but impact that is allowed to remain. Chapter eight will continue this thought. It shows why predictability has become the most important metric. And why YouTube prefers to reward boring consistency over surprising quality.

Notes:

Notes:

Chapter 8: The new currency is predictability

Why predictability is more important than quality today

Quality has long been the promise of the platform. Good content prevails. Bad content disappears. This idea was never entirely true, but it was effective enough to provide guidance. Today, this promise has shifted. It is not quality that determines visibility, but predictability. And predictability is not an aesthetic criterion, but a systemic one. Predictability means that content does not generate surprises that the system cannot classify. It does not mean that content has to be boring. It means that its effect is predictable.

YouTube no longer asks whether content is good, but whether it behaves reliably. Reliability is measurable. Quality is not. High-quality content can trigger many things: enthusiasm, irritation, doubt, reflection. This diversity is valuable to humans, but systemically unsettling. Predictable content triggers less, but what it does trigger is stable. Stability is what platforms prioritize when they have to manage billions of users at the same time. YouTube has learned that quality is no guarantee of stability. On the contrary. Very good content often generates strong reactions. Strong reactions are difficult to control. They lead to peaks, discussions, polarization. All of this increases variance in the system. Variance is the enemy of prediction. Prediction is the basis of control.

Predictability allows for control. A predictable channel generates similar states among similar users. These states can be classified. They can be repeated. They can be monetized. Quality, on the other hand, is uneven. It fluctuates. It surprises. It breaks patterns. It is precisely these breaks that constitute quality. And it is precisely these breaks that are systemically problematic. Many creators experience this conflict as a devaluation of their work. They invest time, thought, creativity. They produce content that is better than before. And yet their reach does not grow. This experience is frustrating, but it can be explained. Quality alone is no longer a criterion for scaling. Predictability seems banal, but it is powerful. A predictable channel is a safe space for YouTube. It produces no surprises. It does not destabilize usage paths. It fits into existing clusters. This fit is crucial. Content is not evaluated in isolation, but in the context of what happens before and after. YouTube measures predictability through repetition. Repetition of themes.

Repetition of tonality. Repetition of effect. A channel that reliably produces similar conditions is read as stable. Stability opens up scope. Not large, but constant. Surprising quality, on the other hand, produces fluctuations. A video performs significantly better or worse than expected. These deviations are exciting from a creative point of view. From a systemic point of view, they are disruptions. Disruptions are not rewarded. They are observed, contained, sometimes corrected. That doesn't mean surprise is forbidden. It just has to be embedded. Surprises are allowed to happen as long as they don't upset the overall state. A single strong video is not a problem. A series of unpredictable content, on the other hand, is. AI does not respond to individual events, but to patterns. Many creators try to increase quality without stabilizing their impact. They increase complexity, depth, and emotionality. These increases are humanly understandable, but systemically risky. If you want to grow, you not only have to get better, but also more predictable. This statement seems cynical, but it describes reality. Predictability is therefore not a call for mediocrity. It is a call for consistency. Consistency in attitude. Consistency in rhythm.

Consistency in impact. Within this consistency, quality is possible. Outside of it, it is limited. Understanding why predictability is more important than quality today changes the view of growth. Growth does not come from content that shines, but from content that carries. Support means that it does not challenge the system, but rather relieves it. This relief is rewarded. The next section shows why YouTube prefers to reward boring consistency over surprising quality. And why this preference is not an expression of taste, but of necessity.

Why boring consistency is considered safer than surprising quality

Boring is not a judgment, but a state. It does not describe the content, but its effect. Boring content demands nothing. It does not irritate. It changes little. That is precisely why it is systemically valuable. Surprising quality, on the other hand, demands attention, presence, and processing. It interrupts routines. And every interruption is a risk. YouTube does not evaluate content according to cultural value, but according to systemic load. Boring consistency hardly creates any load. It generates consistent usage. Consistent usage can be planned. Surprising quality, on the other hand, creates fluctuations. Fluctuations are difficult to predict. Predictability is what large systems must avoid. Consistency has a calming effect. Users know what to expect. They don't have to make a decision. They click because it's familiar. This familiarity reduces cognitive load. Reduced cognitive load increases dwell time. Dwell time in stable states is economically valuable. That is why consistency is preferred, even if it is unspectacular in terms of content.

Surprising quality demands attention. Attention is limited. It is a scarce commodity. Content that demands intense attention exhausts users more quickly. Exhaustion leads to abandonment.

Abandonment is a negative signal. AI responds to these signals not morally, but functionally. It dampens what exhausts too often. Many creators put everything into surprise. They want to stand out. They want to be different. They want to be better than others. But it is precisely this differentiation that creates comparison problems. The system does not know where to classify this content. It does not fit into existing patterns. This mismatch leads to cautious playback. Boring consistency always fits. It is connectable. It fits in. It does not generate discussions, strong emotions, or breaks. It may mean little to the individual. For the system, it is ideal. It keeps the flow going. YouTube therefore prefers channels that reliably deliver similar content. Not because this content is better, but because it is predictable. Predictability allows for automation. Automation reduces costs. Cost reduction increases scalability.

This chain is not creative, but it is logical. Surprising quality can exist within this consistency, but it must not dominate. It must be embedded. A surprising thought in a familiar format is acceptable. A constantly surprising channel is not. The system tolerates deviation as long as it does not become the norm. Many creators perceive this preference as a devaluation of creativity. They feel compelled to repeat themselves. This repetition is indeed a structural constraint. But it is not absolute. There is room for maneuver within the repetition. This room for maneuver lies not in the form, but in the details. In nuances. In depth within consistency. Boring consistency is therefore not an end state. It is a framework. A framework that allows for controlled impact. Those who accept this framework can use it. Those who reject it will be limited. This choice is not fair, but it is real. Understanding why boring consistency is considered safer than surprising quality helps to reduce frustration. It explains why some channels grow despite low innovation. And why others stagnate despite high quality. It's not about better or worse. It's about sustainable or risky. The next section will show how creators can still enable development within this consistency. Not through disruption, but through shift. And why this shift is the only form of innovation that will work reliably from 2026 onwards.

How development remains possible within consistency

Consistency does not mean stagnation. It means recognizability. Development only becomes problematic when it breaks this recognizability. This is precisely where the crucial difference between rupture and shift lies. A rupture destroys expectations. A shift changes them slowly. YouTube reacts to ruptures with caution. It reacts to shifts with tolerance. Development within constancy is a question of speed. Not what changes, but how quickly. Systems tolerate slow change better than fast change. Slow change does not cause fluctuations. It allows for adaptation. Users can follow without being irritated. AI recognizes this adaptation as stable. Many creators believe that development must be visible to be real. They show change openly, abruptly, radically. This openness is humanly understandable, but systemically demanding. A sudden change in tone, attitude, or content creates uncertainty. Uncertainty is limited. Not because development is wrong, but because it is too fast.

Shifts, on the other hand, operate below the threshold of perception. They change accents, not the whole. A thought becomes a little deeper. A perspective a little broader. A language a little clearer. These changes are easier for the system to integrate because they do not force new clusters. They expand existing patterns instead of replacing them. YouTube reads development not in terms of content, but statistically. As long as the conditions a channel creates remain similar, development is allowed. Content can become more complex as long as it does not overwhelm. It can become more personal as long as it does not destabilize. This balance is challenging, but it is possible. Many of the most enduring creators develop in exactly this way. Looking back, you can see clear changes. At the moment itself, they are barely noticeable. This invisibility is not a shortcoming. It is the reason why the development is sustainable. It allows for depth without creating a break. Consistency acts as a container. A lot can happen within this container. The container remains the same. The content changes. This separation is crucial. Anyone who changes the container risks visibility. Those who change the contents remain integrable. The container consists of recurring elements. Tonality. Rhythm.

Length. Attitude. These elements provide orientation. They signal security. Within this security, new thoughts can take effect. Without this security, new thoughts are seen as a risk. Many creators confuse consistency with repetition. They believe that they have to repeat themselves in terms of content in order to remain visible. But consistency does not mean what, but how. Content can be new as long as its effect remains familiar. This distinction is central. Development within consistency requires patience. It requires trust in small steps. It requires a willingness not to make everything visible immediately. This attitude contradicts the logic of quick success, but it corresponds to the logic of sustainable impact. YouTube indirectly rewards this form of development. Not through explosion, but through stability. Channels that develop slowly are not slowed down. They are supported. This support is unspectacular, but it is reliable. Understanding why development within consistency remains possible relieves creators. It shows that they don't have to choose between growth and development. They just have to learn to shape development differently. Not as a break, but as a shift. The next section reveals why these shifts often remain invisible. And why it is precisely this invisibility that is the reason why they work.

Why invisible changes are more effective than visible breaks

Change does not have to be seen to be effective. On the contrary. The more visible a change is, the more closely it is scrutinized. Visibility generates attention. Attention generates evaluation. Evaluation generates risk. Invisible changes bypass this cycle. They work quietly, but they work deeply. That is precisely why they are systemically preferred. YouTube does not respond to intentions, but to effects. A visible break immediately generates measurable effects. Deviating click patterns. Changed watch time. Irritated comments. These signals are read as instability. The system reacts defensively. It dampens reach to limit the deviation. Invisible changes, on the other hand, do not generate clear fluctuations.

They change the effect without destroying the pattern. Invisible change does not mean deception. It means dosage. A thought is not replaced, but expanded. An attitude is not replaced, but deepened. This deepening is noticeable to the viewer, but not irritating. It feels organic. Organic development is accepted because it does not force a decision. Visible breaks demand decisions. Should I stay or go? Should I agree or disagree? These decisions cost energy. Energy is limited. Systems that are designed for the long term avoid unnecessary decision-making requirements. Invisible changes reduce this burden. They allow adaptation without disruption. Many creators believe that development is only honest when it is openly displayed. They explain their changes, mark transitions, and emphasize new beginnings. This transparency is humanly understandable, but systemically risky. It draws attention to the change itself rather than the content. Change becomes an event. Events are scrutinized. Invisible changes, on the other hand, allow change to take place in the background. The content is in the foreground. Development is implicit. Viewers adapt without consciously noticing. This adaptation is more stable than conscious decision-making. It is less reversible. What has been integrated unnoticed is rarely rejected. AI recognizes this integration as continuity. Conditions remain similar. Usage patterns do not change abruptly. Growth remains possible. The creator develops without risking visibility. This form of development is demanding because it requires patience.

It dispenses with the need to mark change. Invisibility is therefore not a weakness. It is a strategy. Not in a manipulative sense, but in an integrative one. It respects the limited adaptability of systems and people. It allows for development without creating excessive demands. Many major changes in stable systems happen in exactly this way. Not through revolution, but through evolution. Not through rupture, but through shift. This logic applies not only to platforms, but also to organizations, cultures, and individuals. YouTube is a system of this kind. Understanding why invisible changes are more effective than visible ruptures helps creators avoid sabotaging their development. It shows that you don't have to be loud to change. That you don't have to explain everything to stay authentic. That impact does not depend on visibility. The next section concludes this thought. It's about why predictability is not the end of creativity, but its new condition. And why creators who accept this become not poorer, but freer.

Why predictability is not the end of creativity

Predictability is often understood as the opposite of creativity. As stagnation. As repetition. As capitulation to the system. But this idea falls short. Predictability is not the end of creativity, but its new condition. In a regulated environment, creativity no longer arises from rupture, but from precision. Not from explosion, but from design. Creativity in a stability-oriented system shifts its focus. It no longer lies in the surprise effect, but in the depth of execution. Not in the what, but in the how. A predictable framework can support an infinite number of variations. The decisive factor is how consciously this framework is used. Those who merely repeat it become rigid. Those who shape it remain alive. YouTube does not demand creative poverty. It demands creative discipline. Discipline here does not mean restriction, but focus. A clear framework reduces possibilities, but it sharpens expression. This sharpening is the place where new forms can emerge. Not through volume, but through precision. Many of the greatest creative achievements have been created within narrow limits. Musical styles. Literary forms. Architectural systems. Limits have never prevented creativity. They have channeled it. Predictability is one such limit. It forces you to become more precise. More refined. More conscious.

Creators who accept predictability stop working against the system. They also stop censoring themselves. Instead, they begin to play within the framework. They use repetition to build depth. They use consistency to reveal nuances. It is these nuances that create impact. Predictability also protects against overload. It relieves the creator of the pressure to constantly be new. Novelty becomes variation, not obligation. This relief creates space for genuine exploration. For research. For maturation. Creativity takes time. Time arises where pressure decreases. Many creators experience a paradoxical effect when they reach this point. They feel freer, even though they are more formally limited. This freedom arises from clarity. Clarity about what the framework is. Clarity about where there is room for maneuver. Uncertainty binds energy. Clarity releases it. YouTube indirectly rewards this form of creativity. Not through viral peaks, but through stability. Stability enables longevity. Longevity allows for development. Development is at the core of any serious creative work. Without longevity, creativity remains episodic. With longevity, it becomes effective. Predictability also means that the audience knows what to expect. This certainty creates trust. Trust allows for depth. Depth is what sustains creativity in the long term. Without trust, creativity remains superficial because it constantly has to fight for attention. Understanding why predictability is not the end of creativity, but its new condition, changes the inner attitude toward the system. The system is no longer experienced as an adversary, but as a framework. A framework that can be used without submitting to it. Chapter eight ends here because a central change of perspective has taken place at this point. Creativity and stability are no longer opposites. They are interdependent. Those who understand this can not only survive in a regulated platform landscape, but also shape it. Chapter nine will continue this line of thought. It shows why the myth of community no longer holds water. And why loyalty alone is no longer a guarantee of growth.

Notes:

Notes:

Chapter 9: The Myth of Community

The myth of community and why loyalty no longer guarantees growth

The idea of community was long one of YouTube's strongest promises. It suggested closeness in the masses, connection despite distance, loyalty beyond algorithms. Creators should not only have viewers, but people who stay, react, defend, and spread the word. This idea was not wrong, but it has become historical. What once enabled growth now has a systemic limiting effect. Not because community has lost its value, but because loyalty is interpreted differently in a stability-oriented platform economy than it was in the past. Bonding creates consolidation. Consolidation creates isolation. Isolation reduces permeability. For a system that depends on permanent circulation, it is precisely this consolidation that becomes problematic. YouTube has learned that strong communities do not automatically generate growth, but often the opposite. They bind attention locally instead of passing it on. They stabilize existing reach but prevent expansion. This effect is subtle but measurable. A community is not a neutral construct. It creates expectations, behavioral norms, implicit loyalties. Viewers who see themselves as part of a community consume content differently.

They compare less, switch less often, and are reluctant to leave familiar spaces. For the creator, this is ideal at first. However, this creates a problem for the platform. Attention remains bound. It no longer circulates freely. Yet it is precisely this free circulation that is the basis of algorithmic distribution. YouTube favors content that enables transitions. Content that users move on from, rather than stay with. Moving on does not mean abandoning, but rather passing through. A video should lead to the next state, not to a closed field. Communities, on the other hand, create fields. They close. They create inside and outside. This demarcation is socially valuable, but difficult to integrate systemically. The myth of community is based on a misconception. Loyalty is equated with growth. In reality, loyalty is a stabilizer, not an accelerator. It holds what is there, but attracts little that is new. New viewers immediately sense the density of a community. They read implicit codes, insider references, and established dynamics. This density is off-putting, not inviting. It signals belonging, but also exclusion.

YouTube measures these effects not ideologically, but behaviorally. New viewers stay for shorter periods of time. They comment less frequently. They return less often. These signals are interpreted as lower connectivity. However, connectivity is crucial for scaling. Content must be open, not closed. Communities tend to be closed, even if they see themselves as open. Many creators misunderstand this connection because the feedback from the community is intense. Comments are long, personal, affirmative. This intensity is interpreted as success. But intensity is no substitute for reach. It can even limit it. A channel with a strong community generates deep resonance but low permeability. For the system, this is an endpoint, not a waypoint. YouTube responds to strong community structures with caution. Not by devaluing them, but by exercising restraint. Content is not aggressively recommended because it is seen as too specific. It suits one group, not many.

This specificity is valuable to humans, but algorithmically limiting. Algorithms prefer content with a low entry threshold. Communities raise this threshold. Loyalty also changes expectation dynamics. A community expects consistency, repetition, and confirmation. Deviations are more strongly sanctioned. The creator is more closely watched and less free. This internal dynamic often leads to a narrowing of content. Content is tailored to the existing group, not to new viewers. Growth continues to slow down.

A cycle emerges. YouTube recognizes this cycle over time. Channels with high community density show stable but limited growth curves. These curves are considered safe but not scalable. The system does not intervene, but it also does not open up new spaces. The channel is managed, not expanded. The myth of community thrives on the confusion of proximity with relevance. Proximity feels relevant because it is emotionally intense. But relevance in a systemic sense means connectivity across contexts. Content must work without prior knowledge. It must be inviting, not familiar. Communities create familiarity. Familiarity is comfortable for existing viewers, but a hindrance for new ones. This does not mean that communities should disappear. It means that they are no longer the growth engine they once were. They are a by-product, not a goal. Those who actively build communities often unintentionally reinforce their own limitations. Those who allow communities to emerge without centering them remain more permeable. YouTube now favors content that enables relationships without demanding belonging. Relationships are easy. Belonging is difficult.

Relationships allow people to come and go. Belonging requires a decision. Decisions cost energy. The system wants to save energy. Many creators intuitively sense this shift. They notice that community calls bring less reach. That internal references perform worse. That content that strongly targets the existing group hardly reaches new viewers. These effects are often misinterpreted. People believe that the algorithm punishes closeness. In reality, it favors openness. The myth of community is therefore not a mistake, but a relic. It stems from a time when platforms wanted to grow.

Today, they want to stabilize. Stabilization requires flow, not loyalty. Content should move people, not hold them back. Chapter nine begins with this disenchantment because it is painful. Many creators have built their identity on community. They feel betrayed when reach stagnates. But the problem lies not in the quality of the relationship, but in its structure. Too much closeness closes spaces. Growth needs open doors. The next section makes it clear why even high interaction is no longer an indicator of growth. And why likes, comments, and shares today often mean the opposite of what creators believe.

Why interaction is now limited rather than rewarded

Interaction has long been considered the most visible proof of relevance. Likes, comments, and shares were seen as signs of resonance, as proof that content reaches, moves, and activates people. In the early logic of YouTube, this assumption was correct. Interaction signaled interest. Interest signaled value. Value was reinforced. This chain has not disappeared, but it has changed direction. Today, interaction is no longer a clear signal of growth, but an ambivalent one. And in many cases, it has a limiting rather than an accelerating effect. The reason for this lies not in the interaction itself, but in its effect on usage paths. Interaction interrupts the flow. It demands action. It demands a decision. Every decision creates a break in automated consumption. It is precisely this break that is systemically problematic. Platforms are optimized to minimize decisions, not maximize them. The smoother the transition from one piece of content to the next, the more stable the system. Interaction counteracts this smoothness. A like is a pause.

A comment is an exit from consumption mode. A share is a shift of attention to the outside world. All these actions are valuable to humans, but systemically ambivalent. They show engagement, but they slow down the flow. YouTube not only measures interaction, but also what happens afterwards. And it is precisely this afterwards that is crucial. High interaction is often accompanied by breaks in use. People comment, reflect, discuss. They remain in the video, but they leave the automated path. From a human perspective, this deviation is a success. From a systemic perspective, it is a risk. AI reads these patterns not as quality, but as friction. Friction is not rewarded, but limited. That's why interaction is a double-edged sword today. It shows intensity, but also interruption.

Content with an extremely high comment rate often generates strong emotional or cognitive reactions. These reactions are rarely neutral. They polarize, bind, narrow. The system reacts cautiously to this because such content is difficult to integrate. Many creators observe this phenomenon without being able to classify it. Videos with thousands of comments do not grow further. Discussions explode, but reach stagnates. This divergence between interaction and growth seems paradoxical, but it is consistent. Interaction shows that something is working. Growth requires that this effect is compatible. YouTube now distinguishes between fluid attention and focused attention. Fluid attention moves on. Captive attention sticks. Captive attention is intense, but it blocks circulation. Platforms need circulation to simulate diversity and spread risk.

Captive attention is therefore not scaled. Interaction captures attention. Comments in particular create local density. People read each other's comments, reply, react. The focus shifts from content to social dynamics. This dynamic is valuable for community, but it narrows the space of perception. Content that generates strong social density is less likely to be widely shared because it absorbs attention rather than passing it on. Likes are less problematic, but they are no longer a pure signal of growth either. A like shows approval, but not connectivity. Many likes can mean that a piece of content fits perfectly with an existing group. However, this is not an indicator of scaling. Scaling requires openness, not a perfect fit.

Shares have long been considered the supreme discipline of interaction. Content that is shared should grow. But here, too, the interpretation has shifted. A share shifts attention out of the system. It interrupts internal circulation. For YouTube, this is ambivalent. The content gains visibility, but the platform loses control. Control, however, is the central goal of a regulated system. AI therefore evaluates interaction not in isolation, but relationally. It does not ask how much interaction there is, but in what context. Interaction that supports the flow is acceptable. Interaction that interrupts it is limited. This evaluation is more subtle than before and more difficult to understand. One example is comments that are purely affirmative. Short expressions of agreement, emojis, simple reactions. These forms of interaction hardly interrupt the flow.

They signal engagement without creating strong states. Such interaction is tolerated. In-depth comments, on the other hand, which open up discussions, express doubts, or develop long trains of thought, create friction. They slow things down. They are not penalized, but they limit scaling. Many creators believe that they must actively provoke interaction. They ask questions, solicit comments, and encourage discussion. This practice stems from an old logic. In the new logic, it can be counterproductive. Not because interaction is bad, but because it is misread. YouTube now favors content that generates resonance without forcing a reaction. Resonance manifests itself in silent approval, in return visits, in uninterrupted dwell time. These signals are quiet, but they are scalable. Loud engagement is visible, but difficult to integrate.

Interaction is therefore no longer a reliable indicator of success. It shows depth, not reach. It shows significance, not scaling. Those who confuse interaction with growth are optimizing at the wrong point. They reinforce precisely what limits the system. This does not mean that interaction should be avoided. It just should not be placed at the center. Content may trigger reactions, but it should not be dependent on them. The more content is designed to elicit a reaction, the more it binds attention locally. Local binding is the opposite of flow. YouTube now reads content based on how easily it can be consumed. A good video is one that makes it easy to click on the next one. Not because the content is forgotten, but because it is integrated. Content that has a lasting effect without blocking is ideal. Interaction often blocks this transition. Many creators experience this change as a devaluation of their community work. They have learned that dialogue is important. That closeness counts.

And that's true. But closeness is no longer a growth driver. It is a stabilizer. Growth occurs where closeness is not a prerequisite. Understanding why interaction is now limited rather than rewarded is painful, but liberating. It takes away the pressure to constantly generate reactions. It allows you to create content that has an impact without binding. This freedom is crucial for sustainable work on a platform that no longer amplifies but regulates. The next section reveals why even high watch time is no longer a guarantee of reach. And why YouTube has begun to reinterpret this long-dominant signal.

Why even high watch time is no longer a reliable growth indicator

For many years, watch time was YouTube's central currency. It was considered an objective signal. Proof that content is captivating. That it is relevant. That it is effective. This clarity no longer exists.

Today, watch time is no longer read in isolation. Instead, it is read relationally. Contextually. In relation to the situation. Long dwell times do not automatically mean quality. Nor do they automatically mean success. They are now just one signal among many. A signal that can have different meanings. A user who watches for a long time is not necessarily well integrated. They may just be stuck. Overwhelmed. Emotionally attached. Internally blocked. This is exactly where the old logic of watch time breaks down. YouTube has learned that high watch time is ambivalent. It can indicate quality.

But it can also indicate friction. Content that is highly emotional, polarizing, or cognitively demanding often generates above-average viewing time. Not because it is easy to integrate, but because it is engaging. It leaves questions unanswered. It doesn't resolve tension. It holds attention. This holding is systemically problematic. Because it blocks transitions. Because it slows down usage. Because it creates unstable states. The new interpretation of watch time therefore no longer asks about duration. Instead, it asks about connection. What happens next. Does the user calmly move on? Or do they stop abruptly? Do they remain stable? Or do they tip over emotionally? Watch time without integration is no longer a value. It is a risk. This explains why videos with extremely long playback times are often not scaled further. Even though they look great on paper. A video can hold people's attention for a long time.

And then leave them exhausted. Or internally blocked. Or emotionally charged. Such content generates systemic costs. Because it interrupts the usage path. YouTube does not optimize for individual videos. But for sequences. For flows. For chains of states. That's why content that may be watched for shorter periods of time is preferred. But which enables transitions. Which concludes. Which calms. Which integrates. Many creators experience this change as a paradox. High watch time. But declining recommendations. This paradox resolves itself when it becomes clear how watch time is interpreted today. Not as a performance indicator. But as a stress indicator. Very high watch time can mean that content is too engaging. Too focused. Absorbs too much attention. Such content is difficult to scale. Not because of a lack of quality. But because of a lack of permeability. YouTube implicitly distinguishes between two types of watch time: flowing and blocking. Flowing watch time is part of a continuous stream of consumption. The user watches for a long time. But then moves on without any problems. Blocking watch time leads to pauses. To interruptions. To internal stops. This form is limited. Quietly. Through careful playback. Content with depth and meaning is particularly affected. With strong narration.

It often leads people into a state of reflection. They think. They pause. Humanly, this is valuable. Systemically, it is a break. Platforms can't do much with reflection. It is not scalable. It is individual. It interrupts flow. Watch time is therefore decoupled from reach. Not because it is unimportant. But because it no longer means anything on its own. Only in combination with transitions. With stability. With follow-up behavior. Does it gain meaning. A video with moderate watch time can be more successful. If it is well integrated and if it opens up transitions. Many creators try to counteract this. They extend content. Stretch suspense arcs. They set up cliffhangers. This often exacerbates the problem. Watch time increases. Integration decreases. Attention is captured, but not released. Today, content must be able to let go. Not just hold on. YouTube prefers content with internal closure. Not because it is banal. But because it closes states. Closed states are sustainable.

Open states are risky. Watch time that creates open states is limited. Even with impressive numbers. Watch time has lost its exclusive status. It is necessary, but not sufficient. The overall progress is decisive, and this is hardly visible to creators. Because it is not communicated. It can only be experienced indirectly. Many creators react with frustration. Or self-doubt. Yet they often do something very right. They create impact. But an impact of condensation. Not of expansion. Condensation is not a mistake. But it does not scale automatically. Watch time is no longer a goal. It is a by-product. It arises when content carries weight. Not when it holds on. YouTube today does not measure how long someone stays. It measures how well someone can move on. That is the invisible evaluation. Those who understand this stop chasing watch time. And begin to shape conditions. They no longer ask how long someone stays. But how someone leaves. This question changes everything. The next section reveals why this ability to integrate is the real key to algorithmic openness. And why creators who share impact instead of holding on to it don't lose. But survive.

Why algorithmic openness is more important than loyalty

Loyalty seems like a promise, but in the context of the system, it is a limitation. Because loyalty binds, focuses, and closes, while algorithmic openness enables transitions, distributes, and keeps things permeable, and it is precisely this permeability that is the criterion by which content is read today. Not whether people stay, but whether they can move on, not whether they commit, but whether they move, because movement is what stabilizes the system, while binding localizes it. Loyalty creates an inner pull that collects, condenses, and holds attention. But this collection is ambivalent for the system because it takes attention out of the flow, binds it to one place, and thus reduces the capacity for distribution, and it is precisely this reduction that is the point at which growth ends, even though intensity increases. For intensity is not a scaling value, but an end state. Algorithmic openness, on the other hand, describes a state in which content does not demand that you stay, but allows you to leave, and it is precisely this permission that creates trust. Because it does not force a decision, demand loyalty, or require belonging, but offers a relationship without obligation, and this form of relationship is systemically sustainable. Because it does not block transitions, but accompanies them.

YouTube interprets openness not as weakness, but as stability, because open content generates less friction; it allows users to come, have an impact, and leave without traces of overload, without emotional fixation, without social condensation, and it is precisely this ease that enables scaling. Not because content means less, but because it demands less. Many creators confuse loyalty with trust. But trust does not require commitment; trust arises where content has a consistent effect, without any claim of ownership. Where it is recognizable without being monopolizing, where it shows attitude without demanding belonging, and it is precisely this attitude that generates algorithmic openness because it remains connectable. Loyalty, on the other hand, closes, even if it is friendly. Because it implicitly says, this is our space. Our language, our story, and this implicit marking is read by new viewers. Often unconsciously, as a boundary, not as an invitation. And this boundary reduces throughput, reduces connectivity, and reduces scaling. YouTube measures these effects via transitions, via what happens after the video, whether users go to similar content or break off. Whether they move freely or get stuck, and loyalty creates stickiness because it binds emotionally. While openness creates movement because it integrates. A channel with high loyalty acts like a node.

A channel with high openness acts like a passageway, and systems prefer passageways. Because they distribute load, minimize risk, and simulate diversity, while nodes bundle attention and are therefore systemically harder to carry. Many creators perceive this logic as devaluing their relationship with their audience. But the opposite is true: the relationship is not devalued, it is reinterpreted. Not as ownership, but as permeability; not as attachment, but as accompaniment. And it is precisely this shift that is the key to sustainable visibility. Algorithmic openness does not arise from neutrality, but from clarity. Clarity about attitude, tone, and impact, without translating this clarity into social obligation. Content can be clear as long as it does not become exclusive, it can be deep as long as it does not conclude, it can have an impact as long as it does not hold on. Many creators lose openness because they begin to address their audience instead of addressing the space. They speak to their own, not into the space, and it is precisely this shift that changes the interpretation of the content; it becomes specific, not connectable, local, not permeable, and thus systemically limited.

YouTube prefers content that has an impact without marking who it is for, because this content can dock anywhere; it does not require a preliminary decision. It invites without binding, and this invitation is scalable, while binding is not. Loyalty also reinforces pressure to meet expectations; the audience expects repetition, confirmation, continuity. Deviation is experienced as a break, and this pressure narrows the creator's scope of action. Content becomes more cautious, more specific, less open, and it is precisely this development that further reinforces the limitation. Algorithmic openness counteracts this. Because it does not fix expectations, but keeps spaces open. Development can happen without being explained. Change can be integrated without causing irritation because no fixed affiliation is violated. Many of the most successful channels from 2026 onwards will not be those with the strongest community rhetoric, but those with the highest level of openness. Their content will work equally well for regular viewers and first-time viewers, without adaptation, without simplification, without internal codes, and it is precisely this simultaneity that is rare but crucial. Openness also means that content remains understandable without prior knowledge, not superficial, but self-explanatory. Its depth lies in the text, not in the context; it needs no history, no affiliation, no explanation, and that is precisely why it can grow. Loyalty, on the other hand, needs history, needs repetition, needs memory, and these prerequisites are an obstacle to scaling. Because they create barriers to entry, even if they are emotionally positive. YouTube rewards openness because openness reduces risk. It prevents escalation, polarization, fixation; it allows the system to distribute impact rather than bundle it, and this distribution is the central principle of stability for the platform.

Those who understand this stop staging loyalty. They will begin to enable trust, not through proximity, but through consistency; not through attachment, but through clarity; not through community rhetoric, but through spatial design. Algorithmic openness is not a loss of relationship, but a different form of it. A relationship that does not hold on, but carries; that does not claim, but enables. And from 2026 onwards, this form will be the only one that both works and grows. The next section reveals why this openness gives small channels a structural advantage, while large channels increasingly suffer from their own density, and why, at a certain point, size is no longer an advantage but a burden.

Why size becomes a burden and small channels have a systemic advantage

Size has long been the ultimate goal because it promised power, security, visibility, and influence, but in a regulated platform landscape, this logic is reversed because size means not only reach, but also consolidation, pressure to perform, inertia, and systemic attention. It is precisely this attention that makes large channels vulnerable today, while small channels remain agile, adaptable, permeable, and thus algorithmically more attractive. Not because they are better, but because they cost less. A large channel carries history, community, expectations, routines, and emotional ties. All of this seems stable, but stability does not equal sustainability, because the larger a channel becomes, the more difficult any change becomes. Every shift, every nuance, because it is filtered through thousands, sometimes millions, of individual expectations, and it is precisely these filters that create friction, friction creates friction, and friction is limited by the system. YouTube does not view large channels as a success, but as a responsibility. Because their impact is no longer local, but systemic, a single video can shift discourse, influence moods, change usage paths, and this power demands control. Not morally, but functionally, which is why large channels are more heavily regulated, played out more cautiously, monitored more closely, and expanded more slowly. Small channels, on the other hand, are easy; they don't cause fluctuations, peaks, or massive shifts; their impact remains local, manageable, and integrable.

It is precisely this integrability that makes them attractive. Because they can be tested without risk, they are allowed to grow without the system having to react immediately. Size also creates consistency in expectations; the audience expects repetition, reliability, and confirmation, and deviations are sanctioned more quickly. Not through hatred, but through irritation, through quietly staying away, and this irritation has a double effect. Not only does it restrict the creator's creative freedom, but it also worsens algorithmic readability because usage patterns become more erratic. Small channels do not have this burden; they are allowed to change, experiment, and shift without being immediately observed. Their development is invisible enough to be integrated, and it is precisely this invisibility that is their advantage. Because it allows adaptation without triggering limitations. YouTube favors channels whose growth needs no explanation; small channels grow quietly.

Organically, without headlines, without viral peaks. They generate no questions, no reports, no external effects, and it is precisely this inconspicuousness that is systemically valuable. Because it does not jeopardize stability. Size also attracts external interests, media, brands, criticism, regulation. All these factors increase the density of observation, and with each additional observation, the pressure for predictability increases. Content becomes more cautious, more predictable, less agile, and this lack of movement is not creatively driven, but structurally enforced. Small channels are largely free of this. They can develop depth without being read immediately; they can generate meaning without being systemically relevant. They are allowed to fail without consequences, and it is precisely this freedom that enables development, while large channels often only manage what they have built up. Many creators nevertheless strive for size because it promises security. But this security is deceptive because it comes at the price of dependence.

Dependence on expectations, on numbers, on system reactions, while small channels have less to lose and can therefore dare more without escalating. YouTube reads this risk distribution very carefully, favoring growth where little can be lost and slowing down where there is a lot at stake. Not out of capriciousness, but out of caution, and this caution hits large channels structurally harder than small ones. Size also means that every interaction has a greater impact. Comments, likes, and shares generate larger swings, larger swings mean greater changes in status, and greater changes in status increase the likelihood of limitation. Small channels, on the other hand, operate in a calmer field. The new paradigm thus reverses the old logic: it is not size that generates growth, but growth that generates size, and this growth must be designed in such a way that it remains sustainable.

Small channels have a structural advantage here because they do not yet have to carry, but are carried. Many of the most successful developments from 2026 onwards will therefore not start with the goal of becoming big, but with the goal of becoming clear. Clarity creates openness, openness creates flow, flow enables growth, and size then emerges as a by-product, not as a goal. Those who understand this logic stop idealizing size and begin to cultivate agility. Not through reduction, but through structure; not through adaptation, but through readability. It is precisely this attitude that allows a growing channel to remain agile. Size becomes a burden if it is not managed; small channels have an advantage because they can still lead without being controlled. They operate below the threshold, below the radar, below regulation, and that is precisely where the most sustainable growth occurs today. Chapter nine ends here because at this point it becomes clear that community, interaction, and size are no longer reliable growth factors. They stabilize, but they do not open up. Growth today does not come from binding, but from permeability. Not from volume, but from carrying capacity, and those who understand this can stop pursuing old images of success and begin to become effective in the new system.

Notes:

Notes:

Chapter 10: How Shorts have changed YouTube's DNA

Why Shorts have changed the platform without becoming visible

The real revolution at YouTube took place quietly. It came without a break, without a new interface, without an official announcement. It took place as a shift in internal logic. This shift is called Shorts. Not because shorts dominate as a format, but because they have changed the evaluation standards of the entire system. Shorts are not an additional feature. They are a new measuring instrument. A new reference system. A new pacemaker for states, attention, and predictability. With shorts, YouTube had to reinterpret attention. No longer as a coherent bond, but as momentary responsiveness. Not as dwell time, but as transition speed. Not as depth, but as smoothness. This new interpretation has seeped into the entire recommendation system, even where shorts are not consumed. Systems do not think twice. They standardize logic.

They transfer standards. Shorts deliver this reduction in its purest form. In the world of shorts, what matters is not whether someone stays, but whether someone jumps ship. Not whether someone thinks, but whether someone keeps swiping. Not whether a state arises, but whether no negative state arises. This logic has proven to be systemically superior. It generates maximum flow velocity with minimal load. It is precisely this flow logic that is now the implicit standard for the entire platform. YouTube increasingly evaluates content based on how short-compatible its effect is, even if it is long. This does not mean that content has to be short. It means that it has to be low-state. It must not interrupt the flow. It must not overwhelm. It must not create unframed ambiguity. It must not set an emotional peak that is not closed again. Anything that does not work in the shorts logic is also treated with caution in the long form. Shorts have thus set a new standard. Not in length, but in tolerance threshold. They define how much irritation, how much complexity, how much emotional movement a piece of content can generate before it is considered stressful. This threshold is low. Not because of cultural impoverishment. But because of efficiency.

Billions of states can only remain controllable if they are flat enough to balance out quickly. The particular effectiveness of shorts lies in their consistency. They allow no after-effects. No aftermath. No pause. Every state is closed immediately. Either by swiping on or by repetition. It is precisely this immediate closure that the system loves. Open states are expensive. They cannot be measured. They cannot be classified. They cannot be continued. This logic has quietly transferred to longform. Not as a compulsion, but as a preference. Content that behaves like shorts, even if it lasts twenty minutes, is preferred. It creates small, self-contained micro-states. It leads without demanding. It lets go without losing. It is precisely these qualities that enable reach today. Many creators consider shorts irrelevant because they produce longform. This is a serious mistake. Shorts haven't changed the format. They've changed the scale. They've defined what a compatible state looks like. Calm. Short-lived. Connectable. Free of internal resistance. With Shorts, YouTube has learned that people don't need to be held on to in order to stay. They just can't be disturbed. This realization has shifted the platform's DNA. Away from attachment.

Toward smoothness. Away from depth. Toward integrability. Away from meaning. Toward state neutrality. This state neutrality is not a cultural ideal. It is a systemic one. It allows for maximum scaling with minimal risk. It prevents escalation, polarization, and exhaustion. It makes content comparable, interchangeable, and predictable. This is exactly what a global system needs in order not to collapse under its own weight. Shorts have not made YouTube more colorful, but flatter. Not more superficial in a moral sense, but less stateful. This lack of statefulness is the new currency. Anything that generates too much is slowed down. Anything that generates too little is carried. Many creators are fighting against this development because they feel that something is being lost. Depth. Excitement. Meaning. But the system isn't fighting against depth. It's fighting against uncontrollability. Shorts are the perfect tool for this. Their real power lies not in their reach, but in their standard-setting. They define what is considered acceptable content. This definition has an effect everywhere. In recommendations. In test phases. In reach distribution. If you want to understand YouTube in 2026, you don't have to produce shorts.

But you do have to think in shorts. Not in seconds, but in states. Not in clips, but in transitions. Not in attention, but in resilience. This is exactly where the next big mistake of many creators begins. They believe they have to adapt. But all they have to do is translate. The next section reveals why shorts have not shifted attention, but power, and why this shift in power explains why long-form content is now judged more harshly than ever before, even though it officially remains the heart of the platform.

Why long-form content is now judged more harshly than ever before

Long-form content is still officially considered the core of YouTube, which is precisely why it is now judged more harshly than ever before. Long content creates states that are more intense, more lasting, and more difficult to control than short formats. Shorts have shown the system how stable attention can be when it remains shallow and flows quickly. Longform shows the system the opposite, namely how easily attention can shift when depth is allowed. This difference has changed the evaluation logic. Not visible. But effective. Long-form content is no longer distributed generously. It is scrutinized. Not for quality. But for sustainability. From a system perspective, every long video is a risk. Not for the content. But for the state it creates. The crucial question is no longer whether a video is good. The question is whether it can be integrated.

Whether it supports or interrupts the flow. Whether it releases or binds attention. Longform can captivate people. But it can also block them. It can polarize. It can be emotionally charged. All of this is valuable to humans. Systemically, it is problematic. YouTube does not optimize for individual videos. YouTube optimizes for sequences. For transitions. For continuous use. Today, a long-form video must fit in. It can have an impact, but it must not dominate. It can have depth, but it must not leave any unresolved issues. Content that takes a long time to digest but does not lead anywhere else is carefully limited. Not as a punishment. But as a protective measure. Shorts have set the standard for how little content needs to generate in order to remain viable. Long-form is measured by this standard. Not formally. But functionally. A long video must be short-compatible. Not in length. But in state. It must be able to conclude. It must be able to relieve. It must enable transitions. Many creators experience this development as a devaluation of depth.

But the system does not devalue depth. It evaluates its consequences. Unguided depth creates open states. Open states cannot be scaled. Longform is therefore no longer a sure-fire success. It is a responsibility. It requires structure. It requires guidance. It requires conscious decisions. Depth does not come from length. Depth comes from order. A structured long video is systemically easier than an unguided short video. Because it orders states instead of accumulating them. YouTube prefers long-form content that regulates itself. Content that doesn't want everything. Doesn't show everything. Doesn't leave everything open. Such content grows more slowly. But more steadily. Other content explodes briefly. And then disappears again. Long-form is therefore no longer a privilege. It is a touchstone. Those who can carry it gain reach. Those who overload it are limited. This is not rejection. It is consistency.

Why creators censor themselves without realizing it

The shift in platform logic is not only technical. It is psychological. It changes not only playback. It changes behavior. Many creators today censor themselves without being asked to do so. Not through rules. Not through warnings. But through experience. Through repeated limitations. Through lack of reach. Through subtle feedback from the system. YouTube doesn't say what's wrong. It just reacts. And it is precisely this reaction that shapes decisions. Creators learn very quickly. They sense which content is supported. They also sense which content is restricted. This perception is not rational. It is physical. It manifests itself as hesitation. As toning down. As cautious wording. As omitting depth. As smoothing of edges. This adaptation does not happen consciously. It happens out of a desire to remain connected. Shorts have reinforced this dynamic. They have shown which states are preferred. Calm states. Fast states. States without aftereffects. Creators unconsciously begin to align their long-form content with this. They shorten thoughts. They defuse statements. They avoid ambiguity. Not out of conviction about the content. But out of systemic experience. This self-censorship doesn't feel like censorship. It feels like professionalism. Like conformity. Like maturity. In truth, it is often avoidance. Avoidance of friction. Avoidance of risk. Avoidance of states that the system does not want to support. That is precisely why it is so effective. It doesn't need external pressure. YouTube benefits from this dynamic. Not intentionally. But structurally.

A system that rewards certain situations automatically generates behavior that reproduces those situations. Creators optimize themselves. They reduce themselves. They regulate themselves. The system doesn't have to intervene. It lets it work. This development particularly affects content with depth. Content with attitude. Content with meaning. Anything that cannot be resolved immediately is formulated more cautiously. Anything that creates tension is closed more quickly. Anything that has a lasting effect is shortened. Not because it is wrong, but because it seems risky. As a result, many creators lose something without immediately noticing it. Their language becomes smoother. Their thoughts become more rounded. Their content becomes more compatible. At the same time, they lose their independence. Not abruptly, but gradually. Imperceptibly. Reach becomes more stable. Impact becomes flatter. The system rewards this development in the short term. It creates predictability. In the long term, it creates interchangeability. When all content is low in status, it loses its distinctive character. Creators feel this as an inner emptiness. As a lack of resonance. As the feeling of being visible without having an impact.

This form of self-censorship is not a moral weakness. It is a logical consequence of the platform structure. Those who fail to recognize this are fighting against themselves. Those who recognize it gain room for maneuver. Not by rebelling against it, but by consciously leading. The next section reveals why this silent self-regulation explains why many channels function correctly and yet stagnate internally, and why true differentiation today lies not in becoming louder, but in dealing precisely with friction.

Why differentiation today needs friction

The quiet self-regulation of creators leads to a paradoxical situation. Content works. Channels run smoothly. Reach remains predictable. And yet stagnation sets in. Not visibly, but internally. Many creators feel that their content is correct, but no longer carries weight. They meet expectations. They don't break any rules. However, they no longer generate excitement. This is where the real problem begins. Differentiation does not come from volume. It comes from friction. Friction does not mean provocation. Friction means resistance in thinking. It forces you to take a position. It generates attention that does not immediately flow on. It is precisely this form of attention that is systemically risky. It is difficult to measure. It cannot be integrated immediately. That is why it is treated with caution. Shorts have created an environment in which friction is minimized. Conditions should remain smooth. Transitions should be quick. Content should not generate internal resistance. In this environment, friction seems like a mistake. Like something that needs to be corrected. Creators begin to avoid it.

They choose safe formulations. They round off thoughts. They resolve tensions early on. The result is compatibility without character. But without friction, there is no distinction. Content becomes interchangeable. Channels lose their profile. Reach may remain stable, but impact disappears. The system carries this content because it causes no harm. However, it does not amplify it because it provides no impetus. Growth does not come from security. Growth comes from controlled deviation. Friction means leadership. It shows the system that content is more than just flow material. It shows that a state is being consciously created. Not by chance. Not escalating. But held. It is precisely this attitude that distinguishes rebellion from maturity. Those who create friction indiscriminately are limited. Those who apply friction precisely are integrated. YouTube does not openly evaluate this difference. It becomes visible over time. Content with guided friction grows more slowly.

But it remains. Content without friction grows steadily. But it disappears in comparison. Today, differentiation is no longer an effect. It is a process. A process that requires patience. Many creators try to force differentiation through formats. They change styles. They vary lengths. They experiment with dramaturgy. That falls short. Differentiation does not arise on the surface. It arises in the state that content leaves behind. This state determines whether a channel is remembered or replaced. Shorts have lowered the tolerance for friction. That doesn't mean friction is forbidden. It must be guided. It must be embedded. It must have a framework. Unframed friction acts like escalation. Framed friction acts like authority. Anyone using YouTube in 2026 must understand this difference. Not to become louder. But to become clearer. Differentiation does not come from more energy. It comes from precisely applied tension. Tension that does not destroy. Tension that supports. The next section will reveal why this guided friction forms the foundation of the new growth model and why creators who master it do not work against the system, but grow within its logic.

Why integration has become more important than attention

This development does not end in prohibition. Nor is there a break. There is a shift in priorities. Attention has not disappeared. Its meaning has changed. It is no longer the goal. It is a means that must be used in a controlled manner. YouTube no longer optimizes for maximum attention. The platform optimizes for keeping attention integrable. Integration means that content is not viewed in isolation. It is read as part of a sequence. As part of a usage path. As part of a sequence of states. A video may generate attention. It may arouse interest. It may build suspense. What happens next is crucial. Can the user continue? Does he remain stable? Or does a break occur? Shorts have shown how important this question is. They have proven that content does not have to have a profound effect to be used. It must be smooth. It must be connectable. It must require little internal work. This logic has spread to the entire platform. Integration has become more important than intensity. Many creators continue to work toward attention. They optimize titles. They sharpen hooks. They increase drama. In the short term, this works. In the long term, it creates costs. Attention without integration leads to exhaustion. It creates peaks. It creates waste.

The system responds to this with limitation. Not immediately. But consistently. Integration seems unspectacular. It doesn't create explosions. It creates progress. Content that integrates well grows slowly. But it remains connectable. It doesn't cause breaks. It creates trust. Not emotional. Systemic. YouTube prefers content that fits into the overall flow. Not because it is arbitrary. But because it is sustainable. Sustainability means that a state not only arises, but can be maintained. Over time. Through repetition. Through variation. New growth no longer arises from peaks in attention. It arises from stable integration. Creators who understand this change their perspective. They no longer ask how they can generate more attention. They ask how they can guide attention. This guidance determines whether reach is created or dissipates. Integration requires clarity. It requires closure. It requires conscious transitions. Content does not have to mean less. It must end cleanly. Open states have a profound effect. However, they are difficult to integrate. Closed states have a calming effect. They are systemically valuable. Shorts have established this logic. Not as an ideal. But as a necessity. Billions of parallel states of use can only be controlled if they remain integrable. Attention that is not integrated is limited. Attention that is integrated is sustained. Chapter 10 ends at this point. Not with an evaluation. But with a shift. Shorts have not made YouTube more superficial. They have made the platform more structured. Those who understand this stop chasing attention. They begin to integrate impact.

Notes:

Notes:

Chapter 11: Why attention is a risk today

Why visibility is no longer automatically rewarded

Attention has long been considered the sure path to growth. Those who were seen grew. Those who stood out were shared. Those who generated reach were amplified. This logic has shifted. Attention is no longer a neutral value today. It has become a risk. Not for creators. For the system. YouTube has learned that attention has side effects. It creates momentum. It creates expectations. It creates demands for connection. Attention wants to be continued. It wants to be increased. It wants to be confirmed. That is precisely where the problem lies. Attention escalates. But systems strive for stability. In the past, attention was seen as success. Today, it is seen as a burden. Not all attention can be integrated. Not all visibility is sustainable. Attention can tip the scales. It can polarize. It can emotionalize. It can throw users off balance. These effects are humanly understandable. Systemically, they are dangerous. YouTube does not optimize to generate as much attention as possible. The platform optimizes to keep attention controllable. Attention may arise.

But it must not trigger chain reactions. It must not create conditions that cannot be closed again. That is precisely why visibility is distributed more cautiously today. Many creators experience this caution as unfair. They see high click rates. They see strong reactions. And yet growth remains elusive. This seems contradictory. In reality, it follows a new logic. Attention is no longer evaluated according to intensity. It is evaluated according to consequences. A video can generate a lot of attention. What matters is what this attention leads to. Do users remain stable? Or do they become restless? Do they continue? Or do they break off? Does trust develop? Or does excitement develop? Attention that creates unrest is systemically expensive. It demands compensation. It demands dampening. It demands control. That is why attention is now dosed. Not openly limited. But carefully guided. Content is tested. Reactions are observed. Transitions are measured. Only when it is clear that attention does not produce any side effects is it expanded. Everything else remains locally limited. This development explains why much content explodes briefly and then disappears again. The attention was real. The effect was strong. The consequences were not sustainable. The system does not respond with prohibition. It responds with restraint. Attention is therefore no longer a goal. It is a means that must be guided. Those who generate it uncontrollably are slowed down. Those who make it integrable are supported. This distinction is new. It is not transparent. But it is effective. The next section will show why this new risk logic leads to viral peaks being systematically avoided today and why sustainable growth is emerging more quietly than ever before.

Why viral peaks are systematically avoided

Viral reach has long been considered ideal. A single video explodes. Numbers skyrocket. Visibility seems to take on a life of its own. This image has become deeply ingrained in the minds of many creators. Today, it seems like a relic. Viral peaks are no longer a success for YouTube. They are a risk. A peak creates imbalance. Attention increases faster than it can be integrated. Expectations grow abruptly. Connection demands arise. Users find themselves in a state for which they are unprepared. The system has to react. Not to evaluate content. But to restore stability. YouTube has learned that viral dynamics have follow-up costs. They lead to dropouts. They lead to overload. They lead to polarization. They create pressure on creators and users. These effects are spectacular in the short term. In the long term, they are destabilizing. That's why peaks are read early today. Not by their size. But by their speed. Rapid growth is no longer a sign of quality. It is a warning signal. It shows that attention is not being integrated gradually. But is occurring abruptly. This is precisely what makes it difficult to control. The system responds to such dynamics with caution. It does not further expand its reach. It tests. It dampens. It waits. Not out of rejection.

But out of protection. Viral effects are no longer perpetuated. They are flattened. Many creators confuse this flattening with punishment. They believe they have done something wrong. In reality, they have created something that the system cannot carry forward. Attention was there. Integration was missing. Sustainable growth follows a different logic. It is slow. It is steady. It does not create leaps. It creates progressions. Such progressions are predictable. They can be controlled. They can be stabilized. That is exactly what the system prefers. YouTube no longer rewards explosions. It prefers curves. Curves show control. Curves show connectivity. Curves show that attention is not only generated, but can also be maintained. This logic explains why many channels grow steadily without ever going viral. Their content does not generate peaks. It generates trust. It does not trigger excitement. It triggers continuity. For creators, this feels unspectacular. For the system, it is ideal. Viral peaks do not disappear completely. They lose their significance. They are no longer a goal. They are a side effect. Those who chase them create instability. Those who accept them but do not need them remain viable. Today, attention is managed. It is not maximized. Management means dosage. Management means rhythm. Management means knowing when enough is enough. Creators who understand this are changing their work. They don't build on the one moment. They build on the process. The next section will reveal why this shift from the moment to the process explains why many creators feel they have to be constantly present and why this constant presence has itself become a new risk.

Why permanent presence itself is becoming a problem

With the devaluation of viral peaks, a new pressure is emerging. This pressure is called permanent presence. Many creators believe they have to remain visible in order not to lose out. They post regularly. They respond quickly. They remain constantly active. This strategy seems logical. It is not. Permanent presence no longer generates value. It creates stress. Not only for creators. But also for the system. A channel that is constantly visible creates expectations. It demands attention. It demands connection. This demand must be met. This is precisely where the risk arises. YouTube no longer interprets presence as engagement. Presence is interpreted as a demand. A creator who is constantly present creates continuous states. These states must be integrated. If this is not successful, fatigue sets in. Fatigue is systemically undesirable. The system prefers rhythms. Not duration. It prefers recurrence. Not permanence.

Content may appear. It may have an effect. But it must also be allowed to disappear. Visibility without pause blocks transitions. It condenses attention. It increases costs. Many creators feel this effect. They post more. They see less impact. They increase activity. The reach does not respond. It feels like stagnation. In reality, it is overload. Attention is no longer integrated. It is congested. Permanent presence prevents processing. Users need distance. They need relief. They need time between states. Content that leaves no room is not passed on. Not out of rejection. Out of self-protection of the system. YouTube now prefers channels that allow for breaks. Not out of a lack of activity.

But out of structural maturity. Pauses show control. They show that impact is being measured out. They show that attention is being guided. Constant presence seems like dependency. It signals that a channel without constant visibility is not viable. The system reacts cautiously to this. It prefers to distribute attention where it is not demanded. This logic contradicts many old recommendations. It also contradicts the feelings of many creators. Visibility feels safe. In reality, it no longer is. Today, security comes from rhythm. From repetition. From conscious limitation. Creators who understand this change their behavior. They don't post less out of fear. They post less out of clarity. They let content take effect. They let situations come to a close. They leave space. This space is not a loss. It is a prerequisite for integration. In the next section, we will see why this conscious approach to presence leads to bonds being formed differently today than in the past, and why closeness no longer grows out of frequency, but out of recognizability.

Why closeness no longer arises from frequency

Closeness has long been defined by presence. Those who appeared often were considered close. Those who posted regularly built relationships. This logic has shifted. Today, closeness no longer arises from frequency. It arises from recognizability. Not from duration. But from clarity. People process content differently than they used to. They are constantly surrounded by stimuli. By voices. By opinions. In this environment, closeness does not arise from more contact. It arises from orientation. A creator does not become close because they are constantly visible. They become close because they remain recognizable. YouTube no longer interprets closeness as interaction. Likes, comments, and reactions are no longer a reliable signal. Closeness is demonstrated by returning. By recognition. By trusting in what to expect. This form of closeness is quiet.

It cannot be measured in individual moments. It is demonstrated over time. Frequency creates habituation. Habituation creates numbness. Content loses its effect when it no longer has any distance. Closeness needs contrast. It needs breaks. It needs space for meaning to emerge. Without space, closeness becomes noise.

Many creators confuse closeness with availability. They react quickly. They respond a lot. They are constantly present. This creates activity. But it does not create loyalty. Bonding arises where content is reliable. Where attitude remains consistent. Where impact is recognizable. YouTube prefers this form of proximity. Not because it is more emotional. But because it is more stable. Recognizability creates less friction than constant variation. It creates less expectation stress. It is easier to integrate. A channel that is clearly recognizable does not have to appear constantly. It is remembered. A channel that appears constantly but does not have a clear profile is overlooked. Visibility does not replace identity. Frequency does not replace attitude. This shift catches many creators unprepared. They invest more time. They increase their output. And still lose resonance. Closeness cannot be forced. It arises when content has a clear internal order. YouTube responds to this order. Channels with clear recognizability are distributed preferentially. Not faster. But more sustainably. Closeness is not built. It is allowed. In the next section, it will become clear why this changed closeness explains why community functions differently today than it did in the past, and why loyalty no longer arises through interaction, but through reliability.

Why loyalty is quietly emerging today

Loyalty has long been understood through activity. Comments were considered closeness. Reactions were considered relationships. Community was considered proof. This equation no longer holds true. Today, loyalty emerges quietly. It develops over time. It emerges without visible signs. YouTube no longer reads loyalty in the moment. The platform reads it over time. It's not the volume that counts. It's the return that counts. It's not the conversation that counts. It's reliability that counts. Users don't have to say anything. They don't have to show anything. They just have to come back. Interaction can be deceptive. It is fleeting. It is situational. It is often tied to emotion. Loyalty is different. It is quiet. It is predictable. It develops when a channel delivers what it promises. Not in terms of content. In terms of status. Many creators try to create loyalty. They ask questions. They encourage. They respond. This creates movement. But it does not create stability. Loyalty does not arise from requests. It arises from orientation. People bond with what gives them security. YouTube prefers this security.

Not out of concern. Out of system logic. Reliable channels generate less friction. They cause fewer dropouts. They are easier to integrate. The system recognizes these patterns. It responds to them. Loyalty is therefore no longer an effect. It is a state. A state that does not have to be visible. A state that cannot be explained. A state that is sustained. Channels with this quality do not grow quickly. They grow steadily. Many creators overlook this development. They look at numbers. They look for signals. They interpret silence as loss. In reality, silence is often a sign of stability. People consume. They process. They come back. Today, loyalty arises where content has a clear conclusion. Where it is not overwhelming. Where it does not leave things open. Where it leaves room. This space is crucial. It allows integration. It allows return. YouTube amplifies these channels. Not spectacularly. Not visibly. But reliably. Loyalty is not celebrated. It is used. That is the difference from the old logic. Chapter 11 ends at this point. Attention has not disappeared. It has become more dangerous. Loyalty has not become louder. It has become quieter. Those who understand this work differently. Those who ignore this work against the system.

Notes:

Notes:

Chapter 12: The creator as a behavior provider

Why content must stabilize behavior today

YouTube no longer views creators primarily as producers of content. The platform views them as generators of behavior. This shift is not public. It is functional. Content is now only a means to an end for the system. The end is stability. In the past, it was enough to generate attention. Today, that is no longer enough. Attention must lead to predictable behavior. Users should not just react. They should move calmly. They should continue. They should remain in the system. The creator thus becomes a supplier of states. Not consciously. Not on commission. But structurally. Every video generates behavior. This behavior is read. It is evaluated. It is classified. YouTube doesn't ask what is said. YouTube asks what happens next. Does the user remain calm? Does he remain oriented? Does he remain connectable? Or does unrest arise? Or does a break occur? Creators whose content leads to stable behavior patterns are preferred. Not visibly. Not officially. But consistently.

Content that makes behavior unpredictable is restricted. Not as a punishment. As a correction. This logic explains why a lot of high-quality content doesn't grow. It's interesting. It's deep. It's relevant. But it generates behavior that is difficult to integrate. People stop. They think. They leave the flow. This is problematic for the system. The creator thus becomes part of a larger control logic. Not as an individual. As a function. They no longer just deliver content. They deliver transitions. They deliver rhythm. They deliver calm. This role is new. It is not named. It is not explained. It is assumed. Those who fulfill it grow. Those who ignore it stagnate. Not out of malice. Out of structure. Many creators perceive this development as a devaluation of their work. They feel reduced. They feel instrumentalized. In truth, the yardstick has shifted. Impact is read differently. Not by meaning. By consequence. YouTube is not a cultural project. It is a system. Systems optimize for what keeps them stable. Creators who stabilize behavior are valuable. Creators who destabilize behavior are risky. This realization is uncomfortable.

It contradicts the self-image of many creative people. However, it explains why reach today has less to do with expression than with leadership. Leadership means creating conditions that can be carried forward. The next section reveals why this new role of the creator means that personality is valued differently today than in the past, and why visibility is no longer linked to expression, but to predictability.

Why personality is calculated today

Personality has long been considered a driver of growth. Those who were clearly recognizable became visible. Those who showed attitude built reach. This logic has shifted. Today, personality is no longer a free expression. It is a factor in the system calculation. YouTube does not read personality in words. The platform reads it in the behavior it triggers. Personality is not valued because it is authentic. It is valued because it is predictable. Predictability does not mean boredom. It means stability. A creator with a strong personality generates expectations. Expectations generate patterns. Patterns can be controlled. This is precisely where the difference lies. Personality is welcome when it is reliable. It is limited when it appears erratic. The system favors personalities that do not constantly reinvent themselves. Not because change is bad, but because change destabilizes conditions. A channel that provokes today and reassures tomorrow creates uncertainty. Uncertainty is systemically expensive. Many creators believe they have to stand out to remain relevant. They vary their tone. They change their attitude. They experiment visibly. This generates short-term attention. In the long term, the system loses trust. YouTube treats personality like a profile. A profile must be readable. It must remain recognizable. It must meet expectations. Personality thus becomes an anchor of stability. Not a means of expression. This development changes the role of authenticity. Authenticity is no longer about showing everything. Authenticity is about remaining consistent. Consistency creates calm. Calm creates connectivity. Creators whose personalities are clearly defined are supported.

Not faster. But more consistent. Their reach grows without peaks. Without slumps. The system can count on them. Other creators create friction. They surprise. They irritate. They change visibly. This can be culturally valuable. Systemically, it is risky. Such channels are treated with caution. This does not devalue personality. It functionalizes it. It no longer serves self-expression. It serves orientation. Users should know what to expect. That is the new standard. The next section reveals why this functional interpretation of personality explains why many creators become estranged from themselves, even though they appear successful on the outside, and why this inner rift has a long-term impact.

Why inner alienation costs reach

Many creators appear successful on the outside but feel empty on the inside. This contradiction is not a personal problem. It is a structural consequence of the new platform logic. Those who make themselves permanently predictable often distance themselves from the part that originally created an impact. This distance often goes unnoticed for a long time. It does not immediately show up in numbers. It shows up in experience. When personality is functionalized, distance arises. The creator delivers what is expected. They fulfill a pattern. They repeat a state. It works. But it costs inner connection. Content feels correct. But it no longer feels coherent. It is precisely this inconsistency that has a subliminal effect. YouTube does not read emotions. The system reads consequences.

Inner alienation changes behavior. It changes tone. It changes rhythm. It changes decision-making patterns. Content becomes more cautious. It becomes smoother. It avoids risk. These changes are subtle. But they are measurable. A creator who is no longer connected internally leads states less clearly. He opens less consciously. He closes less precisely. Transitions become sloppy. The effect becomes diffuse. Reach stagnates not because of a lack of quality. It stagnates because of a lack of leadership. Many creators respond to this with more control. They analyze more intensely. They plan more precisely. They optimize more intensively. This exacerbates the problem. Control does not replace connection. It covers it up. The system responds to this cover-up with restraint. Inner alienation is systemically risky. It creates inconsistency. Not in content. In state. Users sense this inconsistency. Not consciously.

But behaviorally. They stay for shorter periods. They return less regularly. They switch more quickly. YouTube recognizes these patterns. It does not reinforce them. Not out of evaluation. Out of caution. A channel that no longer has its own impact is difficult to integrate. It no longer creates clear states. It creates gaps. This dynamic explains why some creators are no longer growing despite stable numbers. They deliver behavior. But without inner guidance. Behavior without guidance is functional. But it is not sustainable. The way out is not in rebellion. Nor is it in conformity. It lies in recalibration. Creators must feel their impact again. Not to express themselves. To clearly lead states. Those who restore this connection work differently. They produce less out of obligation. They make more conscious decisions. They set clearer goals. This clarity is transferred. Not emotionally. Systemically. The next section reveals why this recalibration explains why some creators suddenly start growing again after years of stagnation without changing their formats, and why inner leadership is more effective today than any external strategy.

Why inner leadership is more effective than any strategy

Reach rarely returns through new strategies. It returns when inner leadership becomes effective again. This leadership is not a concept. It is not a plan. It is a state from which decisions are made. YouTube does not respond to strategies. The system responds to consistency. Inner guidance means that a creator knows what state they are creating. Not approximately. Not theoretically. But concretely. They know when to open up. They know when to close down. They know when a thought is enough. This clarity changes behavior. Not visibly. But effective. Many creators believe that growth comes from optimization. In truth, it comes from consistency. Consistency means that content, attitude, and rhythm are in harmony. When this harmony is missing, friction arises in the system. This friction is limited. Inner leadership reduces this friction. It makes behavior predictable. Not boring. But stable. Stability is not stagnation. Stability is a prerequisite for scaling. YouTube only scales what it can carry. Creators with inner guidance have less to explain. They have less to test. They have less to justify.

Their content comes across as clear. Not loud. This clarity carries over to the user path. Transitions become clean. Abortions decrease. Returns become more regular. The system recognizes these patterns. It does not react immediately. It reacts reliably. Reach does not grow in leaps and bounds. It grows steadily. For many creators, this feels unspectacular. For the system, it is ideal. Strategies cannot replace this effect. Strategies work from the outside. Leadership works from the inside. Strategies change formats. Leadership changes decisions. YouTube reads decisions. Not concepts. Many creators confuse leadership with control. Control narrows. Leadership organizes. Control creates tension. Leadership creates calm. Calm is not stagnation. Calm is the ability to integrate. A creator with inner leadership does not constantly adapt. They react consciously. They choose. They leave things out. This reduction is not a loss. It is precision. Precision makes impact sustainable. Reach is created where impact does not fluctuate. Not because it is weak. But because it is guided. YouTube prefers this kind of leadership. Not ideologically. Functionally. The next section will reveal why it is precisely this inner leadership that explains why some creators suddenly grow without becoming louder, and why the system rewards quiet authority more than visible effort.

Why quiet authority has a stronger effect than visible effort

Many creators believe that growth must make effort visible. More energy. More presence. More activity. This logic stems from a time when attention was the central goal. That time is over. Today, it's not effort that works. Today, it's authority that works. Authority does not come from volume. It comes from calmness. It arises when a creator does not seek attention, but carries it. Quiet authority is not evident in appearance. It is evident in the course of events. Content does not have to prove anything. It has to last. YouTube responds strongly to this form of authority. Not because it is spectacular, but because it is stable. Quiet authority creates little friction. It creates trust. Not emotional trust, but systemic trust. The system can count on it. Visible effort has the opposite effect. It signals uncertainty. It signals need. A channel that fights for attention creates pressure. Pressure creates instability. Instability is limited. Not out of rejection. Out of caution. Quiet authority demands nothing. It explains little. It sets. These settings work.

Not immediately. But sustainably. Users orient themselves by them. They know what to expect. They come back. Not out of enthusiasm. Out of trust. Many creators underestimate this effect. They believe they have to show how much they invest. In reality, the opposite is true. The less visible the effort, the greater the authority. YouTube reinforces these channels. Quietly. Reliably. Quiet authority comes from inner leadership. Those who know what state they are creating don't need to mark it. They simply create it. This self-evidence is rare. It is valuable. It is scalable. The system favors channels that don't push. That don't demand. That don't escalate. They deliver behavior that remains calm. This behavior can be integrated. It does not cause any follow-up costs. Chapter 12 ends at this point. The creator is no longer a performer. They are a behavior provider. Not in a moral sense. In a functional sense. Those who understand this role do not lose freedom. They gain effectiveness.

Notes:

Notes:

Chapter 13: Why authenticity is misinterpreted

Why authenticity is no longer a promise of growth

Authenticity has long been considered the antithesis of staging. Those who were genuine became visible. Those who spoke personally gained trust. This logic has shifted. Authenticity has not disappeared. It is interpreted differently. Authenticity is no longer a promise of growth. YouTube does not evaluate authenticity based on intention. The platform evaluates its effect. An authentic expression can create closeness. But it can also create unrest. It can bind. But it can also block. It is precisely this ambivalence that makes authenticity systemically risky. In the past, authenticity was interpreted as a quality. Today, it is interpreted as a variable.

The question is not whether something is honest. The question is what honesty triggers. Does it lead to stability? Or does it lead to escalation? This question is decisive. Many creators confuse authenticity with openness. They show more. They share personal details. They speak without filters. This creates resonance. But it also creates situations that are difficult to integrate. Closeness without boundaries is unstable. The system reacts cautiously to this. Not out of rejection of authenticity. But out of caution. Authenticity without guidance creates open states. Open states cannot be scaled. They require processing. Processing takes time. Time interrupts flow. YouTube therefore prefers a different form of authenticity. Not the spontaneous kind. The guided kind. Authenticity that is framed. Authenticity that has a conclusion. Authenticity that does not demand, but supports. This shift irritates many creators. They feel compelled to regulate themselves. They believe they are allowed to be less themselves. In truth, the system does not demand pretense. It demands clarity. Clarity about what is shown. And what is not. Authenticity is not rewarded today because it is courageous. It is rewarded when it is reliable. Reliability is the new benchmark. It creates trust. Not emotional trust, but systemic trust. The next section will reveal why this functional interpretation of authenticity explains why many personal posts are well received but do not grow, and why closeness without structure limits reach.

Why closeness without structure limits reach

Personal content often generates a strong response. People feel seen. They feel understood. They react. They comment. They stay. And yet the reach does not grow. This contradiction is frustrating. However, it is logical. Closeness without structure creates bonding in the moment. But it does not create sustainability. Personal content opens up a state. If this state is not guided, it remains open. Open states require processing. Processing slows down usage. Slowing down interrupts flow. This is exactly where the system intervenes. YouTube does not evaluate closeness based on intensity. The platform evaluates closeness based on integrability. Closeness is allowed to develop. However, it must not create a burden. Personal openness can become difficult. It can create emotional bonds. It can lead users into states that are not connectable. This is valuable on a human level. Systemically, it is risky. Many creators believe that closeness is good per se. They tell more. They share more. They open up more. In the short term, this creates resonance. In the long term, it creates boundaries. Reach remains local.

Content is not passed on. Not because it is bad. But because it holds too much. Closeness needs guidance. It needs a framework. It needs closure. A personal thought must be able to end. An emotion must be closed again. Without this conclusion, the user remains stuck. The system recognizes this standstill. It reacts with restraint. Structure does not mean coldness. Structure means responsibility. Those who create closeness bear responsibility for what comes after. This responsibility determines scalability. Personal content without structure has an intense effect. Personal content with structure has a sustainable effect. YouTube prefers this sustainability. Not because it is less honest. But because it costs less. Systems only scale what they can carry. Closeness without structure is difficult to carry. Many creators confuse structure with staging. They believe that structure makes things inauthentic. The opposite is true. Structure enables authenticity. It provides a framework.

Without a framework, authenticity becomes overwhelming. This logic explains why many channels with very personal content have a strong core community. And why they still don't grow. Closeness creates loyalty. Structure scales. Both at the same time is rare. But possible. The next section will show why this combination of authenticity and leadership explains why some creators appear authentic without exposing themselves, and why this form of authenticity is systemically preferred.

Why guided authenticity becomes sustainable

Authenticity works when it is guided, not when it is unfiltered. Guided authenticity means that a creator knows which state to open and which to close. It does not arise from restraint, but from responsibility. A personal thought may be visible, but it must have a framework. This framework makes authenticity sustainable. YouTube reacts calmly to this form of authenticity. It creates closeness without binding. It opens without holding on. It allows identification without overwhelming. It is precisely this balance that is scalable. It is not intensity that matters. Guidance matters. Many creators believe that authenticity must be raw. It must show everything. This idea is culturally influenced. Systemically, it is problematic. Rawness creates open states. Open states cost attention. Attention without closure is limited. Guided authenticity, on the other hand, closes the circle. It lets the user move on. Guided authenticity does not mean pretending. It means organizing oneself.

The creator chooses what is shown. They choose when a thought ends. This choice is not a loss of truthfulness. It is a gain in clarity. Clarity creates trust. Trust creates return. YouTube prefers content that provides this clarity. Not for moral reasons. For functional ones. Content that combines authenticity with structure causes fewer breaks. It integrates better into the usage path. It is easier to pass on. This logic explains why some creators come across as very personal without becoming intimate. Their content is moving. It is not overwhelming. It remains close. It remains light. This is not a technique. It is an attitude. An attitude that leads to states. Guided authenticity requires awareness. It requires the creator to be aware of their own impact. Not analytically. Practically. They sense when closeness tips over. They close before it becomes difficult. This sensitivity is rare. It is valuable. It is scalable. The next section reveals why this guided authenticity explains why authenticity in 2026 has less to do with disclosure than with reliability, and why reliability is the platform's new trust capital.

Why reliability has become more important than disclosure

Authenticity today is no longer measured by how much someone reveals. It is measured by how reliable someone appears to be. Disclosure generates attention. Reliability generates trust. YouTube prefers trust. Not emotional trust. Systemic trust. A creator who constantly reveals new things about themselves generates momentum. This momentum is difficult to classify. It changes expectations. It shifts states. A creator who remains reliable generates orientation. Orientation reduces friction. Friction costs reach. Reliability does not mean repetition. It means stability in state. A channel is allowed to evolve. It is allowed to grow. It is allowed to touch on new topics. The key is that the inner tone remains the same. Users should know how content feels, not what it says. This feeling is the real anchor. YouTube reads this stability very carefully. Not in individual videos, but over time. Channels that appear reliable generate fewer dropouts. They generate less irritation.

They are easier to integrate. The system responds to this with expansion. Not quickly. But constantly. Disclosure without reliability appears unstable. It creates closeness in the moment. But it does not create certainty of expectations. Users do not know what to expect. Uncertainty is systemically expensive. It interrupts flows. It creates hesitation. The system avoids this. Many creators believe they must become increasingly personal to remain relevant. In reality, this often causes them to lose their reliability. Content becomes inconsistent. Conditions become unclear. Reach stagnates. Not because of a lack of authenticity. Because of a lack of leadership. Reliability is the new form of authenticity. It is not demonstrated through commitment. It is demonstrated through behavior. A creator who remains clear appears credible. A creator who constantly opens up appears restless. YouTube prefers calm.

This shift is difficult to accept. It contradicts many cultural narratives about visibility. However, it explains why quiet channels grow while loud ones stagnate. Reliability carries further than disclosure. The next section reveals why this reliability explains why some creators achieve maximum impact with minimal personal disclosure, and why authenticity in 2026 has less to do with courage than with discipline.

Why discipline is more credible than courage today

Authenticity has long been confused with courage. Those who showed themselves were considered genuine. Those who opened up were considered credible. This equation no longer holds true. Courage creates visibility. Discipline creates trust. YouTube responds to trust. Discipline means not showing everything. It means setting boundaries. It means dosing impact. A creator who works with discipline does not appear restricted. They appear confident. Confidence is systemically valuable. It creates stability. Stability can be scaled. Many creators believe that restraint means inauthenticity. In truth, it means leadership. Those who decide what becomes visible take responsibility for the state they create. This responsibility makes content sustainable. Content without discipline appears raw. It is intense. But it is difficult to integrate. YouTube prefers content that limits itself. Not out of control. Out of efficiency.

A system that processes billions of states needs reliability. Discipline provides this reliability. It makes behavior predictable. Not boring. But stable. Courage without discipline leads to escalation. Escalation generates attention. Attention generates follow-up costs. These costs are limited. Discipline prevents this escalation. It keeps the impact within limits. The framework makes growth possible. This logic explains why many creators achieve great impact with little personal disclosure. They are not distant. They are clear. Their content opens up states. They also close them again. Users feel safe. Safety leads to return visits. Authenticity in 2026 does not mean showing everything. It means staying true to yourself. Loyalty is not shown in confession. It is shown in consistency. A creator who remains consistent appears credible. This credibility is quiet. But it is strong. Chapter 13 ends at this point. Authenticity has not disappeared. It has changed its form. It has not become louder. It has become more precise. Those who understand this do not lose expression. They gain sustainability.

Notes:

Notes:

Chapter 14: The invisible area below reach

Why channels disappear without failing

Many channels disappear without being visible. They don't crash. They don't lose subscribers. They aren't blocked. They just stop running. Reach remains absent. Growth stops. Everything seems functional. And yet nothing happens anymore. This state is no coincidence. It is not a mistake. It is a separate area in the system. An area below the active reach. This is where channels that work but no longer carry weight end up. YouTube doesn't just distinguish between success and failure. The platform distinguishes between viable and neutral. Neutral channels don't cause any problems. They don't cause any escalation. But they also don't generate any momentum. They are not penalized. They are ignored. This invisible area is difficult to recognize. The numbers seem stable. The content performs correctly. There are no warnings. No feedback.

That's exactly what makes it dangerous. Creators believe they are on the verge of a breakthrough. In reality, they are at a standstill. The reason is not the content. It is the state. These channels generate impact. But no direction. They generate attention. But no movement. Users consume. They do not react further. The system recognizes this standstill. YouTube does not optimize for satisfaction. It optimizes for flow. A channel that does not generate flow is not distributed further. Not out of rejection. Out of indifference. Indifference is the most dangerous state. Many creators respond to this with more effort. They post more frequently. They optimize more. They vary topics. This often exacerbates the problem. The channel remains neutral. It becomes more active. But not more relevant. The invisible area is not a sidetrack. It is a waiting mode.

Channels can leave it. But not through volume. Not through quantity. Only by changing their impact. The next section will reveal why this area explains why many creators feel cut off from the algorithm, even though technically nothing has happened, and why visibility is not being taken away, but rather no longer being granted.

Why visibility is not being withdrawn, but rather no longer being granted

Many creators talk about shadow bans. They talk about blockages. They talk about being cut off. This language is understandable. It describes a feeling. However, it does not describe what is actually happening. Visibility is rarely withdrawn today. It is simply no longer being granted. YouTube does not work with penalties in the traditional sense. The platform works with priorities. Content is not actively suppressed. It is passively not passed on. This difference is crucial. It explains why everything seems normal and yet nothing grows. A channel in the invisible realm does not violate any rules. It does not cause any damage. But it also does not generate any momentum. The system sees no reason to continue playing it. Not out of rejection. Out of a lack of relevance to the flow. Reach is not a right today. It is a resource. This resource is used where it has an effect. Effect does not mean reaction. Effect means movement. Content must shift something. A state. A transition. A sequence. Channels in the invisible realm generate consumption. But they do not generate change. Users look. They remain calm. They move on.

This is not negative. It is neutral. Neutrality is not reinforced. Many creators wait in this state for a sign. For a push. For a moment. That moment does not come. Not because it is denied. But because nothing triggers it. The system only reacts. It does not initiate. This logic is difficult to accept. It contradicts the feeling of having earned something. It contradicts the idea of fairness. However, YouTube does not work with fairness. It works with function. Visibility arises where content makes a difference to the system. This difference doesn't have to be big. It has to be noticeable. It has to have direction. A channel without direction remains static. This explains why many creators work correctly for years without ever breaking out. They deliver content. They deliver quality. They deliver consistency. What's missing is an impulse that goes beyond neutrality. Visibility is not taken away. It is redistributed. Every day. At any time. Those who receive it fulfill a function. Those who do not receive it fulfill no function. This function has nothing to do with morality. It has to do with system logic. The next section will reveal why this logic explains why many creators remain invisible despite professional content, and why professionalism alone does not generate movement.

Why professionalism alone does not generate movement

Professionalism has long been considered a guarantee of visibility. Clean videos. Good editing. Clear thumbnails. Solid content. All of that was true. And still is. But it's no longer enough. Professionalism prevents mistakes. However, it does not generate movement. YouTube rates professionalism as a basic requirement. Not as a growth factor. A professional channel does not stand out negatively. But it doesn't stand out positively either. It works. That's exactly where the problem lies. Function alone does not generate momentum. Channels in the invisible realm are often highly professional. They deliver reliably. They do nothing wrong. But they also do nothing to change the flow. Users consume. They remain stable. They move on. The system sees no reason to expand. Professionalism has a neutralizing effect. It smooths out rough edges. It reduces friction. It prevents escalation. That's valuable. But it's not distinctive. Distinction does not come from flawlessness. It comes from impact. Many creators confuse movement with quality. They believe that better content should automatically be shared. The system works differently. It does not amplify the best. It amplifies the most effective. Effectiveness means that content shifts something. This shift does not have to be loud. It has to be noticeable. It has to have a direction. A professional video without direction remains static. A less perfect video with a clear impact moves people. YouTube responds to this impact. Not immediately.

But measurably. Content that changes things is tested. Content that only stabilizes remains local. Stability is not a mistake. But it is not a growth driver. Many creators increase their professionalism to break out of the rut. They invest more. They continue to optimize. They refine details. The result remains the same. The channel gets better. The reach does not. The invisible area is full of good channels. Of clean content. Of correct work. What is missing is not skill. What is missing is an impulse that goes beyond neutrality. Professionalism is the ticket. It is not the engine. The engine is impact. Impact occurs where content changes something. Not technically. Contextually. The next section reveals why this missing impulse explains why many creators feel they are doing everything right and still not getting anywhere, and why growth today has less to do with skill than with position.

Why position is more important than skill

Many creators are masters of their craft. They edit cleanly. They speak clearly. They deliver reliably. And yet, there is no movement. The reason is not skill. It is a lack of position. Skill shows what someone can do. Position shows what someone stands for. YouTube does not respond to skills. The system responds to orientation. A channel without a clear position does not generate momentum. It works. But it doesn't move anything. Users consume. They understand. They move on. The flow remains unchanged. Position does not mean opinion. Position means state. Content sets a framework.

It organizes perception. It shifts perspectives. This shift is noticeable. Not loud. But clear. Without this clarity, a channel remains neutral. Many creators avoid taking a position. They don't want to lose anyone. They want to remain connected. They smooth out statements. They relativize thoughts. This increases acceptance. It reduces impact. Impact requires clarity. Clarity creates direction. YouTube prefers content with direction. Not because it polarizes. But because it leads. Leadership reduces uncertainty. Uncertainty is systemically expensive. A clearly positioned channel creates predictable states. These states can be integrated. Position is not extreme. It is not provocation. It is a setting. A setting says what is relevant. And what is not. This selection is crucial. It makes content distinguishable. Distinguishability creates movement. Many creators believe that position is a risk. In truth, neutrality is the risk.

Neutrality creates stagnation. Stagnation is not reinforced. Position creates profile. Profile creates return. Return creates reach. The system quietly tests position. It observes transitions. It measures connection. Content with a clear position is not immediately pushed. It is tested. If it passes this test, it is carried. Not explosively. But permanently. Skill without position is interchangeable. Position without skill is unstable. Growth occurs where both come together. The invisible realm is not left behind by more skill. It is left behind by clear positioning. In the next section, it will become clear why exactly these positions explain why small changes can have big effects and why a precise impulse has more impact than any additional optimization.

Why a precise impulse has more effect than any optimization

Many creators try to overcome stagnation with improvements. They optimize titles. They refine thumbnails. They extend content. They shorten content. These measures are logical. But they are ineffective if the fundamental impulse is missing. Optimization reinforces what already exists. It does not change anything fundamental. A channel that is neutral only becomes more efficiently neutral through optimization. A channel without direction does not become more directional through better technology. This is precisely why many attempts are unsuccessful. A precise impulse has a different effect. It does not change the surface. It changes the effect. It makes a clear difference. Not in volume. In meaning. Such an impulse shifts the state that a channel creates. This shift is small. But it is clear. YouTube reacts sensitively to such shifts. Not immediately. Not visibly. But consistently. A clearly set impulse creates connection. It changes how users proceed. It changes what they expect. It is precisely this change that is relevant to the system. Precision means selection. A thought is set. Another is omitted.

One topic is explored in depth. Another is deliberately ignored. This decision creates a profile. Profile creates direction. Direction creates movement. Many creators shy away from this step. They fear loss. They fear rejection. They fear a drop in reach. In truth, it is the only way out of neutrality. Without impulse, everything remains correct. But inconsequential. A precise impulse does not have to provoke. It does not have to polarize. It just has to be clear. Clarity reduces the scope for interpretation. Reduced scope facilitates integration. The system can work better with clarity than with ambiguity. The invisible realm is not left behind through diligence. It is left behind through setting. This setting is not a one-time act. It is an attitude. An attitude that repeats itself. That confirms itself.

That shows itself reliably. Chapter 14 ends at this point. Invisibility is not a deficit. It is a state. This state can be left behind. Not by more. But by clearer.

Notes:

Notes:

Chapter 15: Why distraction beats education

Why learning is systematically disadvantaged

Education has long been considered valuable. Those who imparted knowledge were considered relevant. Those who explained were rewarded. This logic has shifted. Learning has not disappeared. It has been systematically disadvantaged. Not out of contempt. Out of structure. Learning requires effort. It requires concentration. It requires processing. It requires time. All these factors slow down usage. Slowing down interrupts flow. Flow is the central criterion of the platform. Anything that disrupts it is treated with caution. Distraction has a different effect. It demands nothing. It relieves pressure. It creates light-hearted states. Users remain in the system without having to do any inner work. These states are stable. They are connectable. They can be scaled. This is precisely why distraction is supported. YouTube does not evaluate content according to its social value.

The platform evaluates it according to its systemic effect. Education can be valuable. But it can create states that are difficult to integrate. People pause. They think. They leave the flow. This is a problem for the system. Many creators in the field of education experience this limitation. Their content is appreciated. They are praised. They are recommended. And yet they do not grow. This seems paradoxical. In truth, it follows the logic of the platform. Education captures attention differently than entertainment. Learning is an active process. Entertainment is a passive one. Active processes cost energy. Passive processes save energy. Systems prefer processes that require little energy. Not intentionally. For efficiency. Education often creates open states. Questions remain.

Thoughts linger. This aftereffect is valuable to humans. Systemically, it is expensive. Open states cannot be continued directly. They need time. Time interrupts use. Distraction closes states. It leaves nothing behind. Or almost nothing. That is precisely what makes it sustainable. It enables transitions. It allows continuity. Education rarely does this. It wants depth. Depth slows things down. YouTube does not actively limit education. The platform distributes it more cautiously. Content that demands a lot is kept local. Not out of rejection. To protect the flow. Education remains visible. But it is rarely scaled. This logic explains why simple content is often shared more widely than complex content. Not because it is better. But because it costs less. Costs are not evaluated morally. They are reduced. The next section will show why this cost logic explains why even excellently prepared educational content reaches its limits and why knowledge today must be packaged differently in order to remain sustainable.

Why knowledge must work differently today

Knowledge does not fail because of quality. It fails because of form. Not because of content. Because of the state it creates. Education is not limited because it is wrong. It is limited because it is difficult. Difficult in a systemic sense. Not in an intellectual sense. Knowledge requires participation. Participation generates inner work. Inner work slows down usage. Slowing down interrupts flow. Flow is the central stability criterion of the platform. Anything that interrupts it is treated with caution. In the past, understanding was a goal. Today, it is a side effect. YouTube does not optimize for users to take something away. It optimizes for them to be able to move on. Knowledge that has a lasting effect holds on. It binds attention. This binding is not desirable. Many creators try to make knowledge more attractive. They simplify. They shorten. They emotionalize. This only helps to a limited extent. As long as knowledge creates a state that cannot be completed, it remains systemically difficult. Today, knowledge is only viable if it is integrated. Integration means that a thought is complete. That it does not continue to work. That it does not demand more. An integrated thought is calm. It does not disturb the flow. Distraction fulfills precisely this condition. It leaves no open state. It does not demand processing. It leaves the user free. Free here means connectable. Connectability is the benchmark. Education does not lose because it is inferior. It loses because it wants more. It wants understanding. It wants depth. It wants change. Change is risky. Systems avoid risk. That does not mean that knowledge no longer has a place. It means that knowledge must be managed differently. Not as a process. As a setting. Not as an explanation. As orientation. Today, knowledge content must not demand that anyone pause. It can only offer. It must appear complete. Even if it is complex. Even if it is deep. This shift is painful. It contradicts pedagogical ideals. However, it explains why many good educational formats are stagnating. They are correct. They are valuable. They are systemically difficult. The next section will show why this difficulty explains why even highly relevant content hardly grows and why education only scales when it is no longer experienced as learning.

Why relevance alone does not generate reach

Relevance has long been the strongest argument for visibility. What was important was heard. What was socially significant was disseminated. This connection no longer exists. Relevance is not an amplifier. It is a risk. Relevant content demands a position. It demands evaluation. It demands inner movement. It is precisely this demand that makes it systemically difficult. The system does not seek meaning. It seeks stability. Meaning creates change. Change is unpredictable. Much content is highly relevant. It addresses central issues. It provides guidance. It helps people. And yet it remains small. This is not due to a lack of interest. It is due to the effect it has. Relevance binds. Bonding slows things down. Slowing things down disrupts the flow. YouTube does not measure whether something is important. The platform measures what happens afterwards. Does the user remain calm? Or do they get stuck? Do they start to think? Or do they move on? Relevant content often provokes thought. Reflection is a break in the usage path. Distraction avoids precisely this break. It is meaningless in a positive sense. It does not demand a response. It does not demand change. It leaves the user untouched. This characteristic makes it scalable.

Many creators believe they need to emphasize the importance of their content. They highlight relevance. They argue. They appeal. This exacerbates the problem. The clearer the meaning, the more difficult the integration. Relevance must have a different effect today. It must not demand. It must settle. A relevant thought must appear complete. It must not require further work. Only then does it remain viable. This logic explains why seemingly trivial content achieves enormous reach, while in-depth analyses remain limited. Not because depth is undesirable. But because depth requires work. YouTube does not scale work. It scales states. States must be calm. Relevance creates unrest. Distraction creates calm. Calm wins. The next section reveals why this very calmness explains why education only grows when it feels like entertainment, and why this compulsion for lightness is not a cultural judgment, but a systemic one.

Why education only grows when it feels easy

Education does not fail because of its content. It fails because of how it feels. Learning feels like effort. Effort creates resistance. Resistance slows down usage. This is exactly where the logic of the platform comes into play. YouTube prefers content that feels easy. Not because it is superficial. But because it can be integrated. Content can be complex. It just can't feel complex. That feeling is what matters. Not the depth of thought. The lightness of the state. When a user realizes that something is being demanded of them, friction arises. Friction is limited. Not immediately. But reliably. Distraction feels easy. It demands nothing. It allows. It closes states quickly. Education often feels difficult. It raises questions. It requires processing. It leaves follow-up work. This follow-up work is valuable to humans. Systemically, it is problematic. Many creators try to make education more entertaining. They incorporate jokes. They increase the pace. They emotionalize. That can help. But it does not solve the core problem. As long as content is experienced as a learning process, it remains difficult. Difficult means slow. Slow means risky. Education only grows when it is not perceived as learning. It must feel like orientation. Not like effort. A thought may be set. It must not have to be processed. The user must be able to move on without stopping internally. This form of education is rare.

It requires reduction. It requires selection. It requires discipline. The creator must know what to leave out. Even more than what to say. Leaving things out makes education easy. Not simplification. Completion. YouTube responds to this ease. Content that imparts knowledge without requiring work is carried. It does not create a break. It creates clarity. Clarity is connectable. Connectability is scalable. This logic explains why many educational formats only grow when they stop seeing themselves as such. They stop explaining. They start setting. They lead. They don't convince. They organize. The next section will reveal why this form of set education explains why some creators make complex topics big without trivializing them, and why omission is the real key to scaling knowledge.

Why omission is more effective than explanation

The crucial difference between growing education and stagnating education does not lie in knowledge. It lies in how knowledge is handled. It lies in omission. Not in addition. Explanation expands. Omission focuses. Focus creates impact. Many creators believe they have to say everything in order to be correct. They explain backgrounds. They provide contexts. They back up statements. This is technically sound. Systemically, it is difficult. Every additional thought opens up another state. Every open state requires processing. Processing slows things down. Slowing down is limited. Omission closes. It ends a thought. It allows the user to move on. A clearly stated thought has a stronger effect than a complete explanation. Not because it is more correct. But because it is complete. Completion is sustainable. YouTube prefers content that does not require reworking. Not because reworking is bad. But because it interrupts the flow. Content that explains everything stays in the mind. Content that sets things out clearly lets go. Letting go is scalable. This logic contradicts many educational demands. It feels like loss. In truth, it is precision. Precision means knowing what does not need to be said. This decision is demanding. It requires confidence. Uncertain creators explain. Confident creators set. Omission does not mean simplification. It means condensation. A thought is formulated in such a way that it carries weight. Not in such a way that it is complete. Completeness is not a systemic value. Sustainability is. Many successful educational formats work exactly like this. They provide orientation. Not instructions. They give direction. Not justification. They leave room. But not an open state. This difference is crucial. YouTube reacts calmly to this form of education. Content is not celebrated. It is passed on. It does not create resistance. It creates clarity. Clarity is easy. Ease scales. Distraction does not beat education because it is better. It beats education because it demands nothing. Education can keep up if it does the same. Not through superficiality. Through completion. Chapter 15 ends at this point. Education does not lose because it is worthless. It loses because it wants too much. Those who learn to want less are heard.

Notes:

Notes:

Chapter 16: The new growth model from 2026

Why growth is starting quietly today

Growth will no longer be visible in 2026. It will start inconspicuously. It will start without fluctuations. Without peaks. Without clear signals. This is precisely what is confusing for many creators. Nothing is happening. And yet something is shifting. YouTube no longer distributes reach as an event. Reach is created as a process. This process is slow. It is steady. It is difficult to recognize. Growth is not triggered. It is built up. The new model is not based on attention. It is based on sustainability. Content is not pushed because it stands out. It is carried because it is stable. Stable does not mean boring. Stable means integrable. Today, a channel grows when it creates consistent conditions over time. Not identical content.

But identical effects. Users should know how a video feels. Not what exactly happens in it. This feeling is the real anchor of growth. YouTube is testing this effect step by step. Small groups. Repetition. Observation. There is no moment of breakthrough. There is a series of confirmations. Each confirmation increases trust. Not emotionally. Systemically. Many creators are waiting for that one push. For the algorithm moment. That moment never comes. Not because it is denied. But because it is no longer intended. Growth is no longer a leap. It is a curve. This curve is created by repetition. Not by mass. Not by volume. But by reliability. Reliability is rewarded. Not immediately. But sustainably. The new growth model feels slow. And it is. Slow means controlled. Controlled means scalable. YouTube only scales what it can carry. Carrying capacity is the key criterion. Creators who understand this model change their behavior. They don't seek reach. They build impact. They don't optimize for clicks. They optimize for status. This focus changes decisions. Growth begins when a channel stops wanting something. And starts holding on to something. This holding on is invisible. But effective. The next section reveals why this quiet curve explains why many channels appear to stagnate for months and then suddenly grow continuously without any visible change in their content.

Why apparent stagnation is often already growth

Many creators interpret months without visible growth as stagnation. Numbers hardly move. Subscriptions rise slowly. Reach remains steady. This picture seems frustrating. In the new logic, it is often a good sign. YouTube builds trust before it grants reach. This trust is not visible. It does not show up in clicks. It does not show up in comments. It develops in the background. Through repetition. Through stability. Through the absence of risk. A channel that appears to be stagnating is often read intensively. Not checked in the sense of control. Observed in the sense of classification. The system does not ask whether a video works. It asks whether a channel is viable. Viability takes time. A lot happens during this phase. Transitions are measured. Return visits are observed.

Abortions are compared. The system checks whether the effect remains constant. Not strong. Constant. Constancy is the real growth factor. Many creators destroy this phase. They respond to missing signals with change. They switch topics. They change tone. They vary formats. In doing so, they break exactly what is being tested. The stagnation is prolonged. Not as a punishment. As a reset. Quiet phases are not pauses. They are calibration. YouTube compares data. It checks whether a channel remains predictable. Predictability does not mean predictability in content. It means predictability in status. A channel may surprise. But it must not fluctuate.

Fluctuation creates uncertainty. Uncertainty slows down scaling. That's why reach is only expanded when fluctuation decreases. When growth begins, it happens suddenly. In reality, it was prepared months in advance. The curve doesn't rise because something new happens. It rises because nothing unpredictable has happened. Creators who understand this logic persevere. They don't change.

They refine. They reduce. They stabilize. This work is invisible. But it is crucial. Stagnation is often not a sign of failure. It is a sign of testing. Those who pass this test grow. Those who interrupt it start over. The next section reveals why this testing phase explains why many creators only lose reach when they actively try to regain it, and why patience is a strategic factor today.

Why patience is a strategic factor today

Patience was never a factor for success on YouTube. It was considered passive. An excuse. A lack of ambition. This assessment has shifted. Today, patience is an active strategy. Not out of convenience. Out of system logic. YouTube is sensitive to unrest. Unrest is not evident in content. It is evident in behavior. Frequent changes of direction. Overreactions to numbers. Constant adjustments. All of this signals uncertainty. Uncertainty is difficult to scale. Patience does not mean stagnation. Patience means stability under observation. A creator who shows patience sticks to their impact. They maintain their status. They don't change out of fear. This calmness is readable. Not emotional. Systemic.

Many creators lose reach precisely here. They cannot endure a phase. Numbers stagnate. Expectations rise. Pressure builds. The impulse to change something becomes strong. This impulse is understandable. It is often fatal. Change under pressure has a different effect than conscious development. It creates fluctuation. Fluctuation interrupts calibration. The system has to re-read. Trust is not carried forward. It is reset. Patience allows the system to recognize patterns. Repetition creates comparison. Comparison creates certainty. Certainty enables expansion. This chain is slow. But it is reliable. YouTube does not scale experiments. It scales certainty. Certainty does not come from a video. It comes from behavior over time. Patience provides exactly that time. Many creators confuse patience with passivity. In truth, patience is highly active.

It requires conscious decisions. It requires not doing things. Not reacting. Not varying. This restraint is demanding. Patience also means regulating one's own urge for confirmation. Numbers are visible. Impact is not. Those who focus on numbers lose patience. Those who focus on impact persevere. The new growth model rewards creators who can remain calm. Not because they do nothing, but because they don't interrupt what they are doing right. Patience is not waiting. It is leadership over time. The next section will show why this leadership explains why small channels will have an advantage in 2026 and why size today is no longer achieved through speed, but through stability.

Why small channels have a structural advantage

Small channels seem inconspicuous. They have little reach. They attract hardly any attention. That is precisely where their advantage lies. They are under little scrutiny. They pose little risk.

They are easy to read. YouTube prefers to test new effects where the costs are low. A small channel can fail without causing any damage. A large channel cannot. Size increases responsibility. Responsibility increases caution. Caution slows growth. Small channels are allowed to stabilize without having to meet expectations. They are allowed to remain quiet. They are allowed to have a steady impact. This consistency is valuable. It provides clean data. Clean data accelerates trust. Large channels are under pressure. Every deviation is noticeable. Every fluctuation becomes expensive. The system reacts cautiously. Growth is treated conservatively. Stability is protected. Expansion is delayed. Small channels do not have this ballast. They can build impact without having to defend it. They can show patterns without having to explain them. This freedom is structural. The new growth model favors such conditions. Not out of sympathy. Out of efficiency.

It is easier to scale stability on a small scale than to correct large-scale instability. Many creators underestimate this phase. They want to grow quickly. They want to become visible. They skip the build-up. In doing so, they lose the advantage they would have had. A small channel is not a disadvantage. It is a protective space. Those who take advantage of this phase build a foundation. Impact is clarified. Conditions are managed. Rhythm emerges. When reach comes, these foundations will support it. Without breaks. Without setbacks. Large channels have to relearn. Small channels are allowed to learn. This difference is decisive. In 2026, it won't be the loudest who grow. It will be the most stable. The next section reveals why this structural preference for small channels explains why large creators have to reinvent themselves in order not to fail because of their own size.

Why large channels must reinvent themselves

Size has long been a form of protection. Those who were large were carried. Those who had reach kept it. This logic no longer applies. Today, size is no longer an advantage. It is an obligation. A large obligation creates inertia. Large channels create expectations. These expectations must be met. Every deviation has a greater impact. Every mistake costs more. The system reacts cautiously. Growth is not prevented. It is frozen. YouTube protects large channels from instability. This protection acts as a limitation. Reach is maintained. Expansion does not occur. The channel works. It does not grow. This is precisely where the feeling of stagnation arises. Large channels are more difficult to read. They create many parallel states. Different target groups.

Different expectations. Different reactions. This complexity is systemically expensive. Scaling becomes cautious. Small channels deliver clear signals. Large channels deliver mixed signals. The system prefers clarity. Not size. Clarity can be carried. Size must be managed. Many large creators respond with even more activity. More uploads. More formats. More presence. This exacerbates the problem. Complexity increases. Readability decreases. Growth stagnates. Reinventing does not mean changing everything. It means reducing. Large channels must make themselves readable again. They must standardize their impact. They must clarify situations. Not expand. Bundle. This reduction feels risky. It contradicts the instinct to serve everything. That is precisely why it is necessary. Growth does not come from diversity. It comes from clarity. Large channels that rediscover this clarity can grow again. Not quickly. But steadily. Others remain large. Without development. Size without growth is not success. It is stagnation. Chapter 16 ends at this point. Growth from 2026 onwards no longer follows the logic of speed. It will follow the logic of sustainability. Those who understand this will work with the system. Those who ignore it will work against their own greatness.

Notes:

Notes:

Chapter 17: How content can become interesting again

Why interest was long considered a threat

For years, interest was the driving force behind reach. What captivated was shared. What surprised was amplified. This logic has quietly reversed. Interest has not been abolished. It has been regulated. Not because it is undesirable, but because it is difficult to control. Interest generates movement. It draws attention. It opens up internal processes. That is precisely where the risk lies. An interested user is no longer passive. They think. They evaluate. They pause. This is problematic for the system. Stagnation interrupts flow. YouTube has learned that strong interest has side effects. It can escalate. It can polarize. It can create expectations that cannot be sustained. That is why interest has been dampened over the years. Not openly. Structurally. Many creators felt this dampening. Content that used to be popular lost its reach. Not because it got worse. But because it triggered too much. Interest was seen as a burden. Not as a quality. This phase changed the creative field. Content became more cautious.

Statements became more rounded. Edges disappeared. Interest was replaced by reliability. That was functional. But it wasn't lively. In 2026, this logic begins to shift. Not back to the old freedom. But to a new form of interest. A form that is sustainable. A form that does not escalate. A form that is guided. Interest can arise again. It just can't get out of hand. It must be embedded. It must have a framework. Interest without a framework remains risky. Interest with a framework becomes usable. This distinction is new. It explains why some content suddenly grows again, even though it is interesting. Not despite. But because of its guidance. The system recognizes the difference. Interest is no longer evaluated according to intensity. It is evaluated according to progression. Content may arouse curiosity. It may surprise. The decisive factor is whether it releases the user again. Release is the key. Many creators confuse interest with excitement. Excitement wants resolution. Interest wants orientation. Excitement holds on. Interest opens up. It is precisely this difference that determines sustainability. The next section will show why this guided form of interest explains why content can have depth again without losing reach, and why curiosity has a stronger effect today than provocation.

Why curiosity is more sustainable than provocation

Provocation has long been a reliable means of attracting attention. It provokes. It polarizes. It forces a reaction. This effect is powerful. But it is short-lived. Above all, it is expensive. Provocation generates counter-movement. Counter-movement generates escalation. Escalation destabilizes the flow. That is precisely why it is limited today. Curiosity works differently. It opens without forcing. It invites without holding back. It generates movement, but not resistance. Curiosity is a gentle state. It does not require positioning. It allows orientation. It is precisely this characteristic that makes it sustainable. YouTube prefers states that lead further. Provocation holds back. Curiosity lets go. Provocative content creates tension that demands resolution. A curious question creates interest that can be integrated. This difference is crucial. Many creators confuse interest with appeal. They increase volume. They sharpen statements. They exaggerate. In the short term, this attracts attention.

In the long term, it incurs costs. The system responds to this with dampening. Not out of evaluation. Out of caution. Curiosity does not need exaggeration. It arises from openness. A thought is hinted at. A connection is made visible. The user feels invited, not pressured. This invitation is connectable. It allows for transition. Content that generates curiosity does not have to be loud. It has to be clear. Clarity enables orientation. Orientation reduces friction. The system can pass on such content without increasing risk. Curiosity has a long-term effect. It builds relationships, not emotionally, but cognitively. Users come back because they want to understand. Not because they have to react. This return is stable. It can be scaled. Provocation creates peaks. Curiosity creates curves. Curves are predictable. Predictability is systemically valuable. That is precisely why the assessment is shifting. 2026 is not the year of escalation. It is the year of invitation. Content can be interesting again. Not by fighting. But by leading. The next section reveals why this curiosity-based leadership explains why depth is possible again without costing reach, and why interest grows when it doesn't demand attention.

Why depth is possible again when it is guided

Depth has long been a risk. It demanded time. It demanded attention. It demanded inner movement. That is precisely why it was limited. Not out of rejection. Out of caution. Depth creates states that are difficult to integrate. This logic is beginning to shift. Depth has not disappeared. It was used incorrectly. Unguided depth overwhelms. Guided depth organizes. This difference is decisive. Depth can emerge again when it does not bind, but carries. Guided depth means that a thought does not get out of hand. It is opened. It is held. It is closed. The user does not stand still. They move on. Depth is experienced. Not processed. That is precisely what makes it sustainable. Many creators confuse depth with complexity. They explain a lot. They link everything. They leave nothing open and nothing closed. This creates density. But no guidance. Density without guidance seems heavy. Heavy things are limited. Depth needs reduction. One thought is allowed. Others are deliberately omitted. This selection is crucial. It creates clarity. Clarity makes depth easy. Easy depth is scalable. YouTube responds positively to such content. Not visibly. Not with peaks. But with stability. Content with guided depth is calmly conveyed. It does not create breaks. It creates orientation. The user does not feel challenged. They feel understood. This feeling is crucial. Understanding without effort is the core of sustainable depth. The user takes something away without stopping. Many creators believe that depth must show everything. In truth, depth must know when it ends. A good idea does not need proof. It needs a conclusion. This conclusion makes it integrable. Guided depth requires discipline. It requires restraining one's own ambitions. Not saying everything. Not explaining everything. This restraint is not a loss. It is precision. Depth will not return in 2026 through volume. It will return through guidance. Those who can guide depth do not lose reach. They gain trust. Trust is sustainable. The next section reveals why it is precisely this guided depth that explains why content can once again generate resonance without destabilizing the system, and why resonance does not have to be loud to be effective.

Why interest grows when it demands nothing

Interest does not arise where it is demanded. It arises where it is allowed. Content loses its impact when it demands something from the viewer. Attention. Approval. Reaction. Positioning. Every demand creates pressure. Pressure creates resistance. Resistance interrupts flow. YouTube is sensitive to this resistance. Not morally. Functionally. Content that demands something creates unrest. Unrest is difficult to integrate. That is why such content is treated with caution.

Not banned. Muted. Interest grows when content doesn't demand anything. It shows. It sets. It organizes. The viewer is allowed to watch. They are allowed to move on. They don't have to do anything. This freedom is crucial. Freedom creates openness. Openness is connectable. Many creators believe they have to actively generate interest. They build hooks. They promise added value. They ask questions. In the short term, this creates excitement. In the long term, it creates fatigue. The system recognizes this fatigue. It responds with restraint. Content that demands nothing comes across as confident. It doesn't have to explain itself. It doesn't have to justify itself. This self-evidence creates trust. Trust is the basis for sustained interest. YouTube prefers content that doesn't impose itself. It's easier to share. It causes fewer dropouts. It generates less backlash. Interest is allowed to develop. But it must not be forced. This logic explains why some content grows quietly. It makes no offer. It presents an idea. Those who accept it stay. Those who do not accept it move on. The system interprets this movement as healthy. Interest is not an effect. It is a state. A state that arises when there is no pressure. When there are no expectations. When there is no evaluation. Content that enables this state has a deeper impact than any dramaturgy. Chapter 17 ends at this point. Content can be interesting again. Not because it becomes louder, but because it stops wanting something.

Why minimal irritation has a stronger effect than provocation

Provocation aims for a reaction. It wants approval or rejection. It forces people to take a position. This mechanism is old. It is loud. It is predictable. Above all, it is expensive. Provocation generates a counter-reaction. Counter-reaction generates escalation. Escalation destabilizes the flow. That is precisely why it is limited. Minimal irritation has a different effect. It does not demand a decision.

It does not force a stance. It opens a small gap in thinking. This gap is not threatening. It is curious. The user remains in the flow. But they remain alert. It is precisely this alertness that is valuable.

YouTube is sensitive to this difference. Content that provokes is read quickly. Its effect is clear. Its consequences are risky. Content with minimal irritation has a slower effect. Its impact unfolds over time. Its consequences are sustainable. Minimal irritation can be an unfamiliar thought. A slightly shifted perspective. A sentence that is not immediately resolved. It is important that this irritation remains guided. It must not tip over. It must not demand. It must only mark. Many creators overestimate the strength needed to create an impact. They increase the volume. They sharpen their statements. They polarize. This generates attention. But it does not generate integration. Minimal irritation generates integration. It remains in the system. This form of friction is precise. It requires sensitivity. The creator must know how much deviation a piece of content can bear. Too little has no effect. Too much causes abandonment. This is precisely where the art lies. YouTube tests this balance. Not visibly. Not with clear signals. But consistently. Content with well-measured irritation is passed on. It creates memories. It creates return visits. It creates growth.

Minimal irritation is quiet. It doesn't stand out. It stays. Provocation stands out. It passes. The system prefers what stays. Not what explodes. The next section reveals why this precise dosage explains why content with attitude is possible again without losing reach, and why attitude doesn't have to be loud to be effective.

Notes:

Notes:

Chapter 18: The strategy of intelligent friction

Why complete smoothness prevents growth

For years, smoothness was considered the ideal. Content should be easy to consume. Transitions should be fluid. Resistance should disappear. This logic was necessary. It created stability. It enabled scaling. It made YouTube big. But it is precisely this smoothness that is beginning to limit growth. A system that allows no friction creates no differentiation. Everything feels the same. Everything seems interchangeable. Users remain calm. But they don't remember. Smoothness maintains flow. However, it does not create direction. Growth needs direction. YouTube recognizes this effect. Not openly. But structurally. Content that is completely smooth does not cause any problems. But it also does not generate any momentum. It stabilizes. It does not expand. The system carries it.

It does not amplify it. Intelligent friction works differently. It does not interrupt the flow. It marks it. It creates a moment of orientation. Not of blockage. A thought easily contradicts. A perspective shifts. The user remains internally present without standing still. It is precisely this form of friction that is valuable. Friction becomes problematic when it escalates. When it provokes. When it polarizes. That is the old logic. The new logic works more precisely. It creates small resistances. Resistances that lead. Not fight. Many creators avoid friction altogether. They don't want to lose anyone. They want to remain compatible. The result is neutrality. Neutrality is maintained. It doesn't grow. Growth occurs where something is minimally different. Different enough to be noticed. Not different enough to be disruptive. Intelligent friction is not a stylistic device. It is an attitude. The creator consciously decides where they don't want to be smooth. They put forward a thought that doesn't immediately make sense. They leave a perspective standing without explaining it. This approach generates attention without pressure. YouTube reacts cautiously positively to such content. It is not pushed. It is tested. The test does not ask for approval. It asks for connection. Can users continue with this friction? Do they stay calm? Or do they break off? If content passes this test, it is integrated. Not spectacularly. But sustainably. Intelligent friction creates memory. Memory creates return. Return creates growth. The next section reveals why this particular form of friction explains why some content sticks without polarizing, and why minimal irritation is more effective than any provocation.

Why minimal irritation is more effective than provocation

Provocation aims to elicit a reaction. It wants approval or rejection. It forces people to take a position. This mechanism is old. It is loud. It is predictable. Above all, it is expensive. Provocation generates a counter-reaction. Counter-reactions generate escalation. Escalation destabilizes the flow. That is precisely why it is limited. Minimal irritation works differently. It does not demand a decision. It does not force a stance. It opens a small gap in thinking. This gap is not threatening. It is curious. The user remains in the flow. But they remain alert. It is precisely this alertness that is valuable. YouTube reacts sensitively to this difference. Content that provokes is read quickly. Its effect is clear. Its consequences are risky. Content with minimal irritation has a slower effect. Its effect unfolds over time. Its consequences are sustainable. Minimal irritation can be an unfamiliar thought. A slightly shifted perspective. A sentence that is not immediately resolved. It is important that this irritation remains guided. It must not tip over. It must not demand. It must only mark. Many creators overestimate the strength needed to create an effect. They increase volume. They sharpen statements. They polarize. This generates attention. But it does not generate integration. Minimal irritation generates integration. It remains in the system. This form of friction is precise. It requires sensitivity.

The creator must know how much deviation a piece of content can bear. Too little has no effect. Too much causes abandonment. This is precisely where the art lies. YouTube tests this balance. Not visibly. Not with clear signals. But consistently. Content with well-measured irritation is passed on. It creates memories. It creates return visits. It creates growth. Minimal irritation is quiet. It doesn't stand out. It remains. Provocation stands out. It passes. The system favors what remains. Not what explodes. The next section reveals why this dosage explains why content with attitude is possible again without losing reach, and why attitude does not have to be loud to be effective.

Why attitude is possible again without losing reach

Attitude was long considered a risk. Those who took a clear position were considered vulnerable. Those who committed themselves lost touch. This assumption arose from a time of escalation. Today, it is shifting. Taking a stand is possible again. But only if it is guided. Taking a stand does not work through volume. It works through clarity. A clear stance creates orientation. Orientation calms. Calmness makes connection possible. It is precisely this connection that changes the evaluation of taking a stand in the system. YouTube does not respond to opinions. The platform responds to consequences. A stance that escalates generates a counter-movement. Counter-movement generates unrest. Unrest is limited. A stance that takes effect without fighting appears stable. Stability is supported. Many creators confuse stance with confrontation.

They believe that being clear means being loud. That is a mistake. Clarity comes from precision. A clear sentence can achieve more than any escalation. Precision reduces room for interpretation.

Reduced room for interpretation facilitates integration. A guided stance leaves room. It does not force. It marks. The viewer may agree. They may disagree. They may move on. This freedom is crucial. Freedom prevents defensiveness. Defensiveness is systemically expensive. YouTube prefers content that shows stance without exerting pressure. It creates profile. Profile creates recognizability. Recognizability is sustainable. Stance is not punished. It is functionalized. Many creators avoid taking a stance for fear of losing reach. In reality, they lose impact. Neutrality seems safe. It is not. Neutrality does not generate momentum. Stance generates direction. Direction is necessary for growth. The new strategy is not to tone things down. It is to lead. Stance can be visible. However, it must be complete. A thought is put forward. It is not defended. This sovereignty is more powerful than any argument. Taking a stand without a fight is rare. It requires inner clarity. It requires confidence in one's own impact. It is precisely this quality that the system recognizes. Not ideologically. Structurally. The next section will reveal why this sovereign stance explains why friction does not divide but unites, and why intelligent friction creates closeness instead of distance.

Why friction creates closeness instead of distance

Friction is often confused with separation. With division. With distance. This idea stems from escalating friction. Intelligent friction works differently. It creates closeness. Not despite resistance, but because of it. Closeness does not arise from agreement. It arises from orientation. Content that makes a clear statement shows attitude. This attitude acts as a point of reference. Users don't have to agree with it. They have to understand it. Understanding creates closeness. Friction shows that a creator means something. Not everything. Not arbitrarily. This seriousness is perceived. It creates respect. Respect is the basis of closeness. Not agreement. Agreement is fleeting. Respect is stable. YouTube responds positively to this form of closeness. It is calm. It is not emotionally charged. It does not generate resistance. Users feel addressed. Not pressured. This approach is connectable. Intelligent friction demands attention. But it does not demand a reaction. The user is allowed to nod internally. Or disagree internally. Both are allowed. This freedom prevents defensiveness. Defensiveness destroys closeness. Many creators try to create closeness through commonality. They seek consensus. They avoid tension. This creates harmony. But no bond. Bonding occurs when something meaningful is shared. Meaning arises through setting. Friction shows meaning. It marks that a thought has weight. This weight is felt. Not discussed. This is exactly what makes closeness possible.

The viewer feels taken seriously. Not manipulated. YouTube favors content that creates closeness without binding. Closeness without binding is sustainable. It allows for return. It allows for distance. It allows for freedom. Freedom is systemically valuable. This form of closeness is quiet. It is not visible in numbers. It shows itself in behavior. Users come back. They remain calm. They do not change abruptly. The system reads these patterns. Friction only separates when it fights. When it is guided, it connects. This distinction is central. It explains why intelligent friction is not a risk. It is a tool. The next section reveals why this connecting friction forms the new foundation for sustainable growth and why content without friction loses its impact in the long term.

Why content without friction loses its impact in the long term

Content without friction is pleasant. It doesn't disturb. It doesn't demand anything. It glides through the user path. That is precisely where its weakness lies. What doesn't create friction leaves no trace. It is consumed. It is forgotten. YouTube reliably carries such content. It doesn't cause any problems. It generates stable usage. However, it does not expand the system. Growth does not come from stabilization alone. Growth comes from marked significance. Friction marks significance. It shows that a thought has weight.

Without friction, everything remains equal. Equality creates interchangeability. Interchangeability limits growth. The system cannot recognize any difference. Content without friction does not generate a decision. The user does not have to classify anything internally. They remain passive. Passivity is calm. But it is flat. Flat states can be sustained. But they cannot be expanded. Intelligent friction creates memory. Not through volume. Through position. A thought sticks. Not because it provokes. Because it was set. This setting creates orientation. Orientation creates recurrence. Many creators avoid friction for fear of loss. They don't want to irritate anyone. They want to remain compatible. The result is arbitrariness. Arbitrariness is not punished. It is ignored. YouTube does not respond to niceness. It responds to direction. Direction arises where something is minimally different. Different enough to be noticed. Not different enough to be disruptive. Friction is not an end in itself.

It is a tool. Used correctly, it increases carrying capacity. It creates profile. Profile generates growth. Not quickly. But permanently. Content without friction can be successful. It achieves numbers. It generates reach. In the long term, it loses its impact. It is replaced. It leaves nothing behind. Chapter 18 ends at this point. Intelligent friction is not a risk. It is the prerequisite for content to regain meaning without destabilizing the system.

Notes:

Notes:

Chapter 19: Why small channels have an advantage

Why size is no longer a starting advantage today

Size was long considered an accelerator. Those who had many subscribers gained more reach. Those who were visible remained visible. This logic has been broken. Size is no longer a starting advantage today. It is a factor of inertia. A large channel creates expectations. Expectations create pressure. Pressure creates caution. The system treats large channels defensively. Not out of mistrust. Out of responsibility. Reach that moves a lot must be controlled. Small channels do not create pressure. They do not cause escalation. They have no history that needs to be defended. That is precisely why they are agile. Agility is systemically valuable. It allows testing without risk. YouTube uses small channels as testing grounds. Not officially. Structurally. New effects can be tested there. New conditions can be read there. Failure costs little. Success can be transferred. Large channels are difficult to calibrate.

Every change has a strong effect. Every deviation is expensive. The system reacts cautiously. Growth is conserved. Movement is dampened. Small channels do not have this ballast. They can refine themselves without violating expectations. They can build impact without having to defend it. This freedom is an advantage. Many creators see low reach as a flaw. In the new logic, it is a protective space. Here, clarity can emerge. Here, attitude can grow. Here, rhythm can be found. All this before scaling begins. YouTube prefers this phase. Not out of sympathy. Out of efficiency. Stability is easier to build on a small scale than to repair on a large scale. Small channels provide clean data. Clean data accelerates trust. Size no longer comes from speed. It comes from preparation. Small channels are closer to this preparation than large ones. This reverses the old logic. The next section reveals why this structural agility explains why new creators will be able to grow faster than established ones in 2026, and why experience alone is no longer an advantage.

Why experience is slower than clarity today

Experience has long been considered an accelerator. Those who had been around for a long time understood the system. Those who had produced a lot knew what worked. This assumption is losing its power. Experience is not worthless. It has become difficult. Experience brings patterns. Patterns create habits. Habits create predictability. Predictability is stable. But it is not flexible. The system reacts calmly to stability. It reacts cautiously to movement. Clarity has a different effect. Clarity does not come from repetition. It comes from decision-making. A new channel does not have to unlearn anything. It does not have to correct anything. It can set. This setting is readable. Readability accelerates classification. YouTube prefers clear signals. Not perfect ones. A channel with a clear effect is easier to integrate than a channel with a long history and many deviations. History creates complexity. Complexity slows down scaling. Experienced creators carry baggage. Old target groups. Old expectations. Old formats. Every change is measured against this. The system reacts cautiously. Growth is slowed down.

Not out of rejection. Out of caution. New creators don't have this burden. They start with a clean slate. Every effect counts. Every transition is clean. This cleanliness is systemically valuable. It allows for quick testing. It allows for clear classification. Experience often leads to optimization. Clarity allows for setting. Optimization reinforces the existing. Setting changes the direction. Direction is crucial for growth. Not perfection. Many experienced creators feel slowed down. They work correctly. They deliver consistently. And they don't grow. New creators seem raw. They seem imperfect. And they make a difference. The system responds to this. Experience does not become superfluous. It must be used in a new way. Not as a safety net. As a precision tool. Those who use experience to become clearer win. Those who use it to secure everything lose momentum. Clarity beats experience where the effect is not yet determined. Small channels thrive in this space. Large channels have lost it. That is precisely where the advantage lies. The next section will reveal why this clarity explains why small channels build trust more quickly and why trust is more important today than any history.

Why trust develops faster than loyalty today

Loyalty has long been the goal. Subscribers should stay. Communities should grow. Loyalty should be deepened. This logic is losing its significance. Trust has taken its place. Trust develops faster. And it has a more immediate effect. Loyalty takes time. It requires identification. It requires emotional investment. These processes are difficult. They slow down usage. Slowing down is systemically expensive. YouTube responds cautiously to this. Trust works differently. Trust arises from clarity. A user quickly understands what a channel stands for. They know what to expect. They don't have to commit. They don't have to promise anything. They can come and go. It is precisely this freedom that creates trust. Small channels benefit from this. They don't have overloaded expectations. No conflicting signals. Their impact is manageable. Users can quickly classify them. This quick classification is valuable. It reduces uncertainty. YouTube does not read trust emotionally. It reads behavior. Returning without coercion. Consumption without friction.

Transition without interruption. These patterns show that a channel is viable. Viability is reinforced. Large channels often struggle with loyalty structures. Old promises. Old tones. Old expectations. These bonds seem heavy. Changes are viewed with suspicion. The system reacts defensively. Small channels do not have this burden.

They don't have to keep anyone. They are allowed to lead. Leadership without pressure to commit is effective. It creates trust without obligation. Many creators actively try to build loyalty. They appeal. They demand support. They create closeness. In the short term, bonds are formed. In the long term, costs arise. Trust develops quietly. Without being asked. Trust means that a user feels secure. Not emotionally attached. But oriented. Orientation is connectable. Connectivity is scalable. YouTube prefers this type of relationship. It is easy. It is calm. It is stable. Loyalty can slow things down. Trust speeds things up. The next section reveals why this trust explains why small channels can grow faster when they don't want to hold on to anything, and why letting go is more effective today than holding on.

Why letting go is more effective than holding on

Holding on has long been considered a strategy for success. Viewers should stay. They should subscribe. They should become part of something. This logic created loyalty. But it also created heaviness. Heaviness is systemically problematic. Letting go has a different effect. A channel that holds nothing creates freedom. Freedom creates calm. Calm enables return. The user decides for themselves. They feel no pressure. It is precisely this absence of pressure that is crucial. YouTube responds positively to this freedom. Content that demands nothing causes less resistance. Users move on. They come back. This movement is healthy. It is readable. It is scalable. Small channels benefit from this because they don't have to defend anything. They don't have a community that needs to be retained. No expectations that need to be met. They can set content and let go. This ease is an advantage. Large channels often struggle with holding on. They have to deliver. They have to confirm. They have to meet expectations. This obligation creates tension. Tension is systemically limited. Growth becomes cautious. Letting go does not mean indifference. It means trusting in your own impact. A creator who lets go appears confident. Confidence is attractive. It generates respect. Respect carries further than closeness. Many creators try to hold on to attention. They extend content. They set up cliffhangers. They appeal. In the short term, watch time increases. In the long term, sustainability decreases. The system recognizes this heaviness. Letting go allows transition.

Transition is the central criterion. Not staying. Moving on. Content that allows you to move on is valuable. It fits in. It is carried forward. Small channels that can let go appear larger than they are. Large channels that hold on appear smaller than they are. This reversal is new. It will shape 2026. Letting go is not a weakness. It is a strategy. A strategy that fits the system. Those who do not want to hold on to anything will be carried along. The next section will reveal why this ability to let go explains why small channels not only grow faster but are also more stable, and why stability is more important today than any expansion.

Why stability counts more than expansion today

Expansion has long been the goal. More reach. More subscribers. More visibility. This thinking seems outdated in 2026. Not because growth has become unimportant. But because unsupported expansion is unstable. Stability has become a core value. A stable channel creates predictable conditions. Users know what to expect. The system knows what it supports. This predictability is not a disadvantage. It is a prerequisite for any expansion. Small channels can build stability before expansion begins. They grow slowly. They grow calmly. They grow without disruption. This form of growth is unspectacular. But it is resilient. Resilience is decisive. Large channels often expand before stability is fully established. Old reach meets new expectations. Old formats meet new target groups. This overlap creates tension. Tension limits further growth. YouTube protects itself from unstable expansion. Content that grows too quickly is controlled. Not out of mistrust. Out of risk assessment. Stability allows trust.

Trust allows expansion. Stability is not reflected in numbers. It is reflected in the course of events. Hardly any fluctuations. Hardly any interruptions. Hardly any escalation. This calmness is measurable. Not visible. But effective. Small channels that develop this calmness are prepared. Not celebrated. Prepared. When expansion begins, it seems effortless. In reality, it is the result of long stabilization. Many creators chase expansion. In doing so, they lose stability. In the short term, numbers rise. In the long term, trust breaks down. The system reacts. Growth stops. The curve flattens out. Stability is not a substitute for growth. It is its prerequisite. Without stability, expansion is corrected. With stability, expansion is sustained. Chapter 19 ends at this point. Small channels have an advantage because they have time to become stable before they grow. Those who use this time are not held back. They are prepared.

Notes:

Notes:

Chapter 20: YouTube is not your enemy

Why the idea of a hostile algorithm is wrong

Many creators see YouTube as an adversary. As a force that blocks them. As a system that makes arbitrary decisions. This view is understandable. But it is wrong. YouTube does not act against creators. It acts for stability. The algorithm is not an enemy. It is a regulator. It balances conditions. It reduces risks. It prevents escalation. What feels like a blockade is usually a limitation of instability. Not a rejection of quality. YouTube has no interest in keeping creators small. The platform thrives on content. It thrives on creativity. What it cannot support is unpredictability. Unpredictability costs money. It destabilizes flows. This is exactly where the system intervenes. Many creators interpret these interventions personally. They feel overlooked. They feel treated unfairly.

In reality, the system responds to patterns. Not to people. Not to intentions. To impact. Content is not limited because it is uncomfortable. It is limited because it creates conditions that are difficult to integrate. This differentiation changes everything. It shifts the focus from blame to understanding. YouTube does not optimize against interests. It optimizes for transitions. Anything that blocks transitions is dampened. Anything that enables transitions is supported. This logic is consistent. It is not arbitrary. Those who fight the algorithm are fighting a symptom. Those who understand it are working with the cause. The cause is stability. Not control. Stability is the foundation of a system of this size. Many myths arise from a lack of transparency. YouTube explains little. This creates projection. Projection creates enemy images. Enemy images block learning. Understanding opens up room for maneuver. YouTube is not an opponent. It is a framework. A framework that has become narrower. Not to prevent creativity. To keep it viable. Those who understand this framework lose nothing. They gain freedom within clear boundaries. The next section reveals why this understanding explains why many creators only grow when they stop working against the system and start making their impact systemically readable.

Why growth begins when impact becomes readable

Many creators work against a system they don't understand. They produce more. They optimize harder. They react faster. All of this increases activity. However, it does not increase readability. Readability is the decisive factor. YouTube does not grow through content. It grows through patterns. Patterns arise from repeatable impact. Content can be strong. If its impact cannot be classified, it remains local. The system does not recognize direction. Without direction, there is no expansion. Readability does not mean simplicity. It means consistency in state. A channel may vary. It may surprise. The decisive factor is that the impact remains recognizable. Users should know how a video feels, not what exactly happens. Many creators generate impact without stabilizing it.

Every piece of content has a different effect. Every sound is new. Every impulse stands on its own. That feels creative. Systemically, it's difficult. The system cannot recognize a reliable framework. Growth begins where impact becomes repeatable. Not identical. Repeatable. A state returns. A feeling sets in. This return is measurable. Not for the creator. For the system. YouTube reacts calmly to this return. Content will not explode. It will be integrated. Integration is the crucial step. An integrated channel will be carried forward. Not because it is better. Because it fits. Many creators confuse readability with adaptation. They fear a loss of expression. The opposite is true. Readability protects expression. It makes it viable. Without readability, expression is limited. Readability arises from conscious decision-making. What does this channel want to trigger? What does it not want to trigger? This selection is crucial. It reduces dispersion. It increases clarity. YouTube is not an opponent that needs to be convinced. It is a system that wants to be read. Those who learn to make their impact readable stop fighting. They begin to grow. The next section reveals why this very legibility explains why success in 2026 will have less to do with tricks than with attitude, and why attitude is the most stable growth factor.

Why attitude is the most stable growth factor

Attitude is not a statement. It is not an opinion. It is not an image. Attitude is what remains when everything else varies. That is precisely why it has become the most stable growth factor. YouTube does not respond to individual content. It responds to the internal consistency of a channel. This consistency does not come from the choice of topics. It comes from attitude. A creator with a clear attitude appears predictable in the best sense of the word. The system can support them. Attitude is evident in the way topics are dealt with. In the tone. In the way thoughts are presented and concluded. This style remains recognizable even when the content changes. It is precisely this recognizability that is crucial. Many creators believe that attitude is a risk. They fear restriction. They fear losing touch. In truth, attitude protects against arbitrariness. Arbitrariness is systemically worthless. Attitude creates profile. Profile creates trust. YouTube prefers channels that know what they stand for. Not because the system evaluates opinions. But because clarity reduces costs. Clear channels generate less friction. They are easier to integrate. They cause less escalation. Attitude is quiet. It doesn't shout. It doesn't convince. It's just there. This matter-of-factness is crucial. A creator with attitude doesn't have to explain anything. They come across as consistent. Consistency is measurable. Many slumps in growth occur when attitude is abandoned. Numbers stagnate. Panic ensues. Content is adapted. Attitude is watered down. In the short term, this appears flexible. In the long term, it destroys readability. Attitude is not dogma. It is a framework.

Movement is possible within this framework. Without a framework, every movement becomes arbitrary. The system cannot deal with arbitrariness. In 2026, it will not be the loudest creator who grows. It will be the clearest. Clarity does not come from strategy. It comes from attitude. Attitude is non-negotiable. That is precisely why it carries weight. The next section will reveal why this attitude explains why creators become more successful in the long term when they react less and lead more, and why leadership does not mean control, but direction.

Why leadership is more important than control

Many creators try to gain control. Over numbers. Over formats. Over reactions. Over algorithms. This control is an illusion. YouTube cannot be controlled. It can only be read. And this is exactly where leadership begins. Leadership does not mean determining everything. Leadership means setting a direction. A creator leads when they know what state they want to create. Not when they try to control every reaction. Control creates constriction. Constriction creates tension. Tension is limited. YouTube reacts negatively to attempts at control. Not consciously. Structurally. Content that is visibly optimized appears strained. They want to achieve something. It wants to force something. This desire is legible. It creates resistance. Leadership works differently. It is calm. It is clear. It sets a framework and allows movement. A guided channel knows what it is doing. But it also knows what it is not doing. This clarity creates trust. Trust is scalable. Many creators confuse leadership with dominance. They believe they have to hold on to the viewer. Steer them. Convince them. The opposite is true. Good leadership lets go. It allows for decision-making. It respects autonomy. YouTube prefers this autonomy. Content that allows freedom causes less resistance. Users don't feel manipulated. They remain calm. They move on. This calmness is the key metric. Leadership shows itself in the conclusion. A thought is put forward. It is not defended. It is not expanded upon. It is concluded. This conclusion is crucial. It allows integration. Integration allows scaling. Control wants results.

Leadership enables process. YouTube scales processes. Not results. A channel that can lead remains viable. Even if individual videos fluctuate. Many creators lose themselves in control because they are afraid. Afraid of insignificance. Afraid of stagnation. This fear is understandable. But it is counterproductive. Fear causes unrest. Unrest is limited. Leadership arises from confidence in one's own impact. Not from certainty about the result. Those who lead accept uncertainty. This acceptance is paradoxical. It makes impact stable. The next section reveals why this attitude of leadership explains why sustainable success does not begin spectacularly but ends quietly, and why the last step is not a growth trick but a change of perspective.

Why success ends quietly and doesn't begin loudly

Sustainable success on YouTube doesn't begin with a breakthrough. It ends with calm. This calm is not stagnation. It is not a loss of ambition. It is a sign that a channel has arrived. Not at its destination. In its function. Creators often imagine success as an explosion. As a moment. As visibility. As recognition. These images come from an old platform logic. In 2026, success looks different. Success is when nothing has to be forced anymore. A successful channel seems natural. It needs no explanations. It needs no justifications. It does not react to every fluctuation. It stays true to itself. This naturalness is the end product of the entire journey. YouTube carries such channels calmly. Without peaks. Without drama. Without drawing attention to the process. Reach is created. It remains. It fluctuates little. It is precisely this unspectacular nature that is the real success. Many creators miss this moment. They continue to chase. They continue to optimize. They continue to react. They don't realize that the system is already working. They interpret calm as danger. In truth, it is confirmation. The last step is not a new trick. It is a change of perspective. Away from fighting. Away from convincing. Away from explaining. Towards being. A channel that is, works. A channel that wants to work, disturbs. YouTube is not your enemy. Nor is it your friend. It is a system that seeks stability. Those who provide stability are supported. Not celebrated. Supported. And being supported is more than just being visible. This book has not provided a checklist. No hacks. No shortcuts. Not out of lack. Out of consistency. Shortcuts exist in a system that regulates. What remains is understanding. Those who understand YouTube 2026 stop fighting. They stop demanding. They stop reacting. They begin to lead. Quietly. Clearly. Precisely. And that is exactly where what many are looking for emerges. Reach without struggle. Impact without pressure. Success without noise. This is where the book ends. Not with a promise. With an invitation. Not to defeat YouTube. But to position yourself so clearly that resistance becomes unnecessary.

Notes:

Notes:

Concluding remarks:

Beyond impact

This book does not end with a method, a checklist, or a promise, because all of that would contradict what has become apparent in the last few pages. Impact is not created by adding, but by omitting. Not by volume, but by precision. Not by pressure, but by inner order. Many readers will close this book with a feeling that is difficult to describe. Not euphoric. Not motivated in the classic sense. But calmer. Clearer. Perhaps also more uncomfortable. Because some things that have long been externalized are suddenly back where they belong. With your own impact. With your own decisions. With the question of what can be carried—and what should no longer be carried. This is precisely where the real work begins.

Not publicly visible. Not spectacular. But structural. Where attitude is no longer described, but has an effect. Where content is no longer optimized, but guided. Where reach is no longer pursued, but allowed to emerge. In our daily work with creators, entrepreneurs, media personalities, and organizations, we encounter this moment time and time again. People who know everything technically. Who have understood everything analytically. And who nevertheless sense that the next step is not further input, but an inner clarification of their impact. Not as self-awareness. But as strategic maturity. This is exactly where our consulting comes in. Not with formats. Not with algorithms. Not with interfaces. But with impact systems. With the question of how presence is created without pressure. How reach can grow without escalation. How clarity is created without explaining oneself. How leadership becomes possible without exposing oneself. We don't work on visibility. We work on sustainability. On order. On transitions. On the quiet logic that determines whether a system opens up or limits. This work is not loud. It is not fast. But it is effective. Because it does not work against platforms, but with their deepest structures. If this book has set something in motion without you being able to say exactly what it is, then it has been effective. If you still have questions that cannot be answered with tutorials, then you have come to the right place. And if you feel that it is less about YouTube and more about the way you come across, lead, and hold space, then that is exactly where the work we accompany begins. Not intrusive. Not standardized. But precise. Discreet. And consistently focused on impact. Some paths you have to walk alone. Others become clearer when someone walks with you who doesn't steer, but sees.

That's all it takes.

Günther & Yves Plamenig

Notes:

Notes:

Books by the author:

Title: THE INVISIBLE WALL - Why YouTube blocks you when you become interesting

Title: Health after 50 - Why a healthy metabolism is more important than any diet

Title: PROTOCOL OF EMPTINESS - Realistic science fiction thriller

Title: The Silent Wanderers - The obscure truth

Title: Being Fiction

Title: THE IDENTITY MACHINE

Title: How to build a million-dollar business in one year

Title: You are more than just your thoughts

Title: THE THRUH OUT THERE

Title: The 2% - You decide

Title: The 2% - You decide

Title: El 2% - Tú decides

Title: The New Mental Training 2025

Title: Depth and Clarity

Title: The End of Lies - Why the Truth Doesn't Need an Opinion

Title: THE OTHER YOU - Who Would You Be Without Your History?

Title: Hypnosis as a Path to Myself

Title: Charismatic Communication

Title: Loyalty - How We Recognize Who We Can Trust

Title: The Plamenig Self-Hypnosis Technique

Title: Flash Hypnosis

Title: The True Reality

Title: God Doesn't Have Time for Us Because He Has More Important Things to Do

Title: God Doesn't Need Us

Title: Spirit

Title: The Man with Three Faces

Title: The Mental Coach

Title: The Silent Power - Hypnosis as a Modern Management Tool

Title: The Silent Art of Change – Plamenig Hypnosis

Title: Mentally Strong on the Field – The 5-Step Program for Soccer Players

Title: The Myth of the Battery-Free Car – What Tesla Really Knew

Title: Interest Is the Key to Everything in Life

Title: The Mediator

Title: The New Pope

Title: The Algorithm of Longing – How Machines Read Our Hearts

Title: The Power of the Present – Hypnosis and Mindfulness as a Path to Inner Freedom

Title: Successful Hypnosis – Practice

Title: Modern Hypnosis – Inductions for Addicts

Title: Hypnosis 2025 – New Techniques and Insights

Title: Human 2.0

Title: Heart Time

Title: Who Am I Really?

Title: The Crisis of Meaning in Modernity – Why We Have Everything and Yet Feel Empty

Title: Why Most Relationships End After 9 Months

Title: The First Three Months Unemployed at the RAV

Title: Brain Hacking

Title: 100 Years Young

Title: The Entrepreneur of the Future

Title: How Modern Parents Should Raise Their Children

Title: The Community Advisor

Title: The Board Advisor

Title: The Board Advisor

Title: The True and Right Business Partner

Title: How to Build a Million-Dollar Business in One Year

Title: The Road to Your First Million

Title: The Formula for the Future: AI, Personality, and Business

Title: Unleashing Charisma

Title: The Swiss Building Consultant

Title: The Construction Site Handbook

Title: A Day in the Future

Title: The Presidential Advisor

Title: The Truth Out There – UFOs, Aliens, and the Silence of the Powerful

Title: Paths to Success

Email: bottomupverlag@gmail.com

Sold out in bookstores:

Title: Paths to Success, 1st edition now available again at: bottomupverlag@gmail.com

Price: CHF 35.50 including shipping.

Publisher: Bottom up

Email: bottomupverlag@gmail.com

Books available: Online and in all bookstores!

https://buchshop.bod.de/catalogsearch/result/index/?q=Günther+Plamenig

Order books directly from the publisher:

https://verlag.bottom-up.ch

Notes:

Contact us:

Autor book – web- address:

info@die-unsichtbare-mauer.ch

www.die-unsichtbare-mauer.ch

Personal consultation web-address: Systemic channel reading

info@systemische-kanal-lesung.ch

www.systemische-kanal-lesung.ch

Notes:

Notes:

Notes:

Notes:

Cover image:

MD - stock.adobe.com